# KTOWN & COUNTRY ITCHENS

# EVERYDAY COLLECTABLES

# KTOWN & COUNTRY KITCHENS

**WHSMITH**

EXCLUSIVE
· BOOKS ·

**Editor** Joey Chapter
**Art Editor** Gordon Robertson
**Production** Craig Chubb

Produced exclusively for WH Smith Limited by
Marshall Cavendish Books Limited
119 Wardour Street
London W1V 3TD

Concept, design and production by Marshall Cavendish Books Limited

First printing 1991
1 2 3 4 5 6 7 8 9    99 98 97 96 95 94 93 92 91

Typeset by Litho Link Ltd., Welshpool, Powys, Wales
Printed and bound in Hong Kong

ISBN 1 85435 419 1

Most of this material was previously published in the Marshall Cavendish partwork *Times Past*.

# CONTENTS

# INTRODUCTION

In the past, the kitchen and 'life below stairs' have often been associated more with pain than pleasure – a legacy borne out by long working hours, heavy duties and few amenities which left little time for leisure. Times have changed – and in these days of fast food and the microwave oven, there is a growing desire to look back, with nostalgia, into the 'old-fashioned' kitchens to discover their secrets. Dedicated collectors and those people interested in 'putting back the style' into their homes have long been doing this, but for the new and would-be collector, kitchens of the past provide a tremendous wealth of artefacts that are both affordable and available today.

Many items, ranging from chairs, tables and dressers to preserving pans, biscuit moulds and nutmeg graters, for example, were not only made from local materials but were made to last, and were, on the whole, beautifully hand-crafted with a simplicity that comes from practical necessity – a quality that modern homemakers find particularly attractive.

This charmingly illustrated book covers kitchen styles from the Regency period through to the 1930s, illustrating a formidable variety of collectables from trivets and skillets, cheese dishes, coffee grinders, mixing bowls, food packaging, jelly moulds and irons through to ranges, fireside rockers, rolling pins, recipe books and so on – with glimpses into the Victorian dairy equipped with milk churns and butter-making implements; the Edwardian laundry room, home to the mangle, dolly peg and goffering irons; and through to the 1930s kitchen furnished with the latest in plastic tableware.

From an historical perspective, collecting kitchen antiques can add immeasurably to our understanding of the lifestyles and fashions of previous centuries, and, on a more practical level, they are investments that can be used or displayed to give great visual pleasure. Both the established collector and the newcomer to collecting will find the text stimulating and informative, and the accompanying price guides an invaluable asset when evaluating a purchase price (see the Price Guide below for the key to the price codes used within the book). Useful information is also given on how to identify the work of important craftspeople, recognize makers' marks and distinguish between the genuine and reproduction.

I hope this beautifully produced book will inspire you in your quest for treasures and that it will help you to build up a collection that will bring never-ending pleasure.

**Tony Curtis**

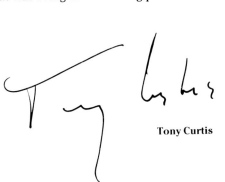

| PRICE GUIDE | |
|---|---|
| **KEY** | ❺ £200-£400 |
| ❶ £15-£30 | ❻ £400-£750 |
| ❷ £30-£60 | ❼ £750-£1500 |
| ❸ £60-£100 | ❽ £1500-£6000 |
| ❹ £100-£200 | ❾ £6,000 plus |

# The Regency Kitchen

## In a large country house the kitchen was of generous proportions and produced an almost constant stream of elaborate dishes

Modern visitors to the Regency kitchen of a stately home are impressed by its cool spaciousness, its large, well-scrubbed tables and dressers, and the vast array of highly polished copper utensils. But although the kitchen was a surprisingly large and lofty room, it was also an intensely busy one with its own mini-climate, blasted by fires and ovens and rendered moist and murky by steam and smoke. The cooks and kitchen maids worked hard from breakfast to supper time, and their task was complicated by the Regency host's insistence on making a show by presenting dishes as elaborately and ingeniously as possible. As in the past, most foodstuffs continued to be home pro-duced, and operations such as the spit-roasting of meat remained essentially unchanged. However, a range of gadgets made the kitchen a more interesting, though hardly a less laborious, place.

The kitchen of a Regency country house was the vital centre of a large servants' quarter. In the country, Regency grandees and gentlefolk preferred to keep their servants out of sight for much of the time, even if this meant locating the kitchen at an inconvenient distance from the breakfast and dining room. Therefore one wing was usually given up to the servants' hall and the laundry, along with the kitchen, the scullery, pantries, larders, china closet and still room (once used for distilling cordials and

# Kitchen Perils

WITH ITS ROARING FIRES AND GUSHING STEAM, THE KITCHEN COULD BE A DANGEROUS PLACE, ALTHOUGH CONTEMPORARIES ALSO SAW THE HUMOROUS SIDE OF KITCHEN LIFE. SERIOUS CULINARY ART WAS IN THE HANDS OF MEN, AND HAVING A FEMALE COOK WAS CONSIDERED A SIGN OF SOCIAL OR FINANCIAL INFERIORITY. LEAVING THE KITCHEN IN THE HANDS OF WOMEN, SO MEN THOUGHT, WAS ASKING FOR TROUBLE. IN GRAND ESTABLISHMENTS HOWEVER MALE CHEFS RELIED HEAVILY ON THE SERVICES OF AN ARMY OF KITCHENMAIDS.

▲ ENTHRALLED BY SIR WALTER SCOTT'S NOVEL, THE COOK IS OBLIVIOUS TO THE DESTRUCTION AROUND HER.

▶ ANIMALS RUN RIOT WHILE THE COOK GESTICULATES HELPLESSLY AND THE MENFOLK LOOK SUPERIOR.

▼ *Even the humblest kitchen items could be lovingly crafted, like this earthenware bread crock.*

◀ *The massive kitchen of the Royal Pavilion in Brighton is the epitome of Regency style, combining space, elegance and practicality in an impressive manner.*

medicines but now adapted to make superior cakes, biscuits and preserves). Here – segregated from the gentlefolk but only a bell-pull away from fresh commands – the servants formed their own hierarchy, headed by the steward or butler, with a housekeeper in charge of the female staff.

The cooks were men, although most of their helpers were women, since they could be paid less than men performing the same tasks. A grand household might have several cooks or chefs, and the Prince Regent himself employed a dozen at his fabulous and lavish new oriental-style palace, the Marine Pavilion (now better known as the Royal Pavilion, Brighton).

## SPACE AND STORAGE

A typical country-house kitchen was a spacious, severely functional room, two storeys high and well lit by one or more windows. The floor was stone flagged and the ceiling was hung with hams, bunches of herbs and crates of bread, kept there out of the way of rats and mice. The walls were often painted blue, since for some reason this was believed to keep off flies. Apart from a few sturdy chairs of the Windsor type, the central area was dominated by very large work tables on which much of the preparation was carried out. The table tops were usually of yellow-white sycamore, which stood up well to years of pounding, chopping and scrubbing.

Open shelves ran round the walls, carrying hundreds – literally hundreds – of gleaming copper saucepans, pots, boilers, kettles, trays and other utensils. The metal was enormously popular despite

contemporary writers' warnings about the dangers of verdigris poisoning. Only towards the end of the Regency period was a safe plating method devised. As protection against this menace – and no doubt to create an effective display – all the kitchen copperware was thoroughly scoured with sand.

## OAK DRESSERS

Also set against the walls were one or more oak dressers. The dresser could be decorative – unlike other kitchen furniture it was sometimes made in the fashionable style of the day – and it was certainly a useful multi-purpose object. Its shelves could be fitted with rails to hold plates, or the pewterware on which the servants themselves often dined. It also provided an extra working surface, beneath which were drawers and a central cupboard used to store table linen, cutlery, glasses, cups and even edibles.

Apart from the dressers, the Regency kitchen – unlike its Victorian counterpart – boasted relatively few cupboards and drawers. Yet order prevailed, as it had to do if large and sometimes indeterminate numbers of people were to be served satisfactorily. Despite the huge amount of equipment employed, most of it was ready to hand, hanging from the hooks and chains fixed to the walls and ceiling.

Regency extravagance did not extend to the servants' quarters, and at Erddig Park 'Waste not' was pointedly written up over one of the kitchen arches. Traditional economies continued to be practised, including the collection and use of dripping – fat that dripped down into a tray from the spit-roast – for candles and rush lights.

The kitchen's focal point was the open-hearthed fire (or, sometimes, fires) set in a wall and burning fiercely behind horizontal metal bars. By the early 1800s the first kitchen ranges – enclosed fires heating metal surfaces – had been introduced, but the open or 'down' hearth remained the norm in country houses. Even in the ultra-modern Great Kitchen, installed at the Marine Pavilion in 1817, both ranges and open fires were used. Wood was still the preferred fuel where available, although deforestation made the use of coal unavoidable in many areas.

Traditionally, the roasting of beef was the central operation in the kitchen. Although British cuisine had become more varied and sophisticated, this aspect of cooking was still important, thanks to the potent symbolism of John Bull and 'the roast beef of Old England'. Roasting was still done on a spit which turned the meat so that it was more or less evenly done, but there was now no need for the services of a boy or a dog to act as turnspit. These had been replaced by ingenious heat-propelled and clockwork-driven jacks. In some places even these were giving way to the Dutch oven, a hooded, curved metal screen that stood in front of the fire and whose polished interior reflected the fire's heat on to the meat while a clockwork mechanism slowly turned it.

In 1748 a Swedish visitor declared roundly that 'the art of cooking as practised by most Englishmen does not extend much beyond roast beef and plum pudding'. If this was ever true, it had ceased to be so by Regency times. As well as roasting, the hearth was used for boiling, baking, steaming and many other operations, while items such as poultry were cooked over separate fires in smaller 'basket' grates.

### A VARIETY OF FOOD

The 18th-century revolution in English agriculture had made vegetables more popular (though it is true that the equation of meat-eating with health and prosperity died very hard). The cultivation of root crops, which made it possible to keep cattle alive throughout the winter, meant that there was more fresh meat available all year round, no longer in need of heavy spices to mask its dubious flavour.

To judge from its sheer variety, the dessert was the Briton's supreme delight. The choice ranged from traditional puddings, fruit and nuts, to syllabubs, sorbets, ice creams, jellies, blancmanges and other smooth, creamy concoctions. As contemporary recipe books and menus make clear, the Regency upper class ate abundantly, variously, and in great style.

### ICY VAULTS

To lighten their labours, the kitchen staff used a surprisingly large number of clever gadgets and devices, including trivets and skillets, down-hearth and salamander toasters, grillers, tongue presses, beer warmers and wafer-irons for making wafers. They even had the benefit of refrigeration, since the winter ice on the estate's ponds and lakes was broken up and kept in deep vaults for cold storage during the summer months. But since their masters and mistresses were more demanding than ever, the cooks and maids were probably really no better off in terms of leisure.

Recipes of the time blithely recommend that an

▲ *The kitchen was a centre of gossip and intrigue, as well as a place of work.*

▲ *This plain but handsome kitchen table is made of cherry wood, a close-grained, richly-coloured wood much favoured by furniture manufacturers. It dates from about 1800.*

egg should be beaten for three hours 'until it be froth', and Regency dinners were regarded as opportunities for extravagant displays in which the provender was presented in various bizarre and fanciful shapes. Fortunately moulds provided many short cuts, enabling cooks to create figures and patterns without excessive labour. Most large kitchens had scores of moulds, ranging from the simplest shapes to classical figures and temples, which were used for a wide range of foods: pies, mashed potato, gingerbread, butter, sugar for decorating cakes, and jellies and blancmanges.

### SOURCES OF SUPPLY

Many of the foodstuffs used in the kitchen came from the estate attached to the country house. Fresh fare from the home farm, kitchen garden, fish ponds and dovecote supplied the kitchen via the buttery, bakehouse, dairy, slaughter house and brewery. Bottling and preserving, pickling, smoking and potting remained important activities, since there was a long winter to get through. The development of the railway network was a few years away, and the country house was still dependent on the carrier and

his horse-drawn waggon. His slow expeditions and infrequent visits did, however, break down the old self-sufficiency of the country house, bringing tea and coffee, loaf sugar, nutmegs and mace, rice and other provisions, all of which helped to make the Regency kitchen a creative, busy place.

▲ *A well-equipped Regency hearth, with its open range and full array of spits and roasting apparatus, is a majestic as well as a welcoming sight.*

# Regency Food

UPPER-CLASS WEALTH AND AMPLE SUPPLIES OF SERVANTS MADE REGENCY COOKING LUXURIOUS, VARIED AND OSTENTATIOUS. THE VOLUME OF PATRIOTIC FULMINATIONS AGAINST FRENCH CUISINE INDICATES THE STRENGTH OF ITS INFLUENCE, AND THE PRINCE REGENT HIMSELF IMPORTED THE FAMOUS FRENCH CHEF CARÊME TO WORK AT THE ROYAL PAVILION IN BRIGHTON. ONE BANQUET THERE IN 1817 FEATURED FOUR SOUPS, FOUR FISH DISHES AND NO LESS THAN 36 ENTREES.

CURRIES AND CHILLIS WERE KNOWN FROM THE 18TH CENTURY, WHEN 'NABODS' WHO HAD MADE LUCRATIVE CAREERS IN INDIA CAME HOME TO LIVE IN STYLE. THE MOCK-ORIENTALISM OF THE ROYAL PAVILION FURTHERED THE FASHION FOR THINGS INDIAN. THE EFFECTS OF INDIAN BURDWAN, BRADO FOGADO AND OTHER EXOTIC CURRY DISHES COULD BE OFFSET BY SUCH COOL PUDDINGS AS ICE CREAMS, SORBETS AND SYLLABUBS.

▲ THE KITCHEN AT BRIGHTON'S ROYAL PAVILION IS TRULY PALATIAL IN SCALE, BEFITTING A ROYAL RESIDENCE.

▲ GOOD COOKING, IN REGENCY TIMES AS ALWAYS, DEPENDED ON A READY SUPPLY OF FRESH INGREDIENTS.

# The Windsor Chair

One of the most popular, adaptable and enduring items
of furniture, the ubiquitous Windsor chair was first
recorded in the early 18th century and is still being
made today

By the early 19th century the well-to-do could choose from a wide variety of furniture styles, made in exotic imported woods as well as indigenous ones. Many of these designs were inspired by the influential style books of eminent furniture designers such as Robert Adam, George Hepplewhite, and Thomas Chippendale Senior and Junior.

Yet even against such competition, the long popular, modestly-priced Windsor chair continued to be held in high esteem. Sturdy yet stylish, easy to lift and move around, it was also remarkably comfortable, thanks to the characteristic saddle-shaped wooden seat. Its arms also added to its comfort, although some chairs in the Windsor style were without arms.

All these qualities made it ideal hard-wearing furniture for country kitchens or hallways, alehouses and gardens.

## WHY WINDSOR?

No-one knows for certain how the chair got its name. Windsor was never a centre of production. One version is that the Prince Regent stopped at a wayside inn, when out riding, and, being seated in the best chair in the house, remarked on its great comfort. Thereafter, so the story goes, it was called the Windsor chair. Romantic perhaps, but the chair was being produced long before his day. A more likely – and more prosaic – explanation is that the finished chairs were transported by river from Windsor to the London shops and markets.

▶ *The timeless appeal
of Windsor chairs
allows them to
harmonize with all but
the most modernistic
kitchens. Here in
Lindisfarne Castle an
18th-century comb-
back shares a kitchen
with a contemporary
elm settle, a later
basketwork armchair
and a Jacobethan
rocker.*

◀ *Their lightness and
hard-wearing qualities
meant that Windsors
were often taken out of
the kitchen to be used
as garden furniture.
Chairs intended for this
purpose were often
painted green.*

The earliest Windsor chairs evolved from the 16th-century turned stool, with which it shared an important design element; the legs, arm supports, back splats, stays and sticks were all inset into the seat. By the late 16th century the turned stool had been given a high back – a simple panel of wood topped by a cross-rail. Then arms were added and by the beginning of the 18th century it had evolved into the more refined and decorative Windsor chair.

## BODGERS, BENDERS AND FRAMERS

By then, Windsor chairs were widely produced in rural areas where suitable timber could be found. The most productive areas were the West Country, the Midlands and particularly Buckinghamshire, where High Wycombe became a main centre. Since making the chairs involved several different craft skills, teams of men worked on them, but not always in the same workshop.

The turners, or 'bodgers', fashioned the spindles, legs and stretchers from wood that was still green. They worked in the woodlands, close by the beech trees marked out for the purpose. With a cross-saw they cut the trunks into chair-leg lengths. Then

dowelled through an arm hoop set halfway down the back and continued on into the seat itself. The legs too, were dowelled into the seat and secured by pegs or tenons. Unlike later designs, these often had no restraining stretchers, so the legs always splayed slightly.

When stretchers were featured, these were a simple H-shape until the 1740s, when the curved crinoline or cow-horn stretcher became common. These later chairs sometimes had a central splat with fretted decoration or carving. Some mid-century chairs also had cabriole legs, though these can often look somewhat at odds with the saddle-shaped seat. Cabrioles were already going out of fashion on other chair styles and by 1770 they were used less and less for Windsors. Between 1780 and 1800, baluster-shaped legs with attractive decorative turnings appeared on some comb-back designs.

One of the most striking designs was the 1760s Gothic Windsor with a Gothic arched back and several back splats – sometimes side-arm splats too – with 'church window' style piercing. They are now very rare, and highly prized.

### BOBTAILS

To strengthen the chairback, some 18th-century Windsor chairs featured a tailpiece known as a 'bobtail' and bracing sticks that descended diagonally from either end of the top rail or comb to meet in a V-shaped support at seat level. There, they were mortised into the bobtail seat extension.

they used a wooden mallet, known as a beetle, and a splitting-out axe to cleave the lengths into rough leg shapes, after which the ends were roughly tapered before further refinement with a shave horse, then a pole-lathe.

The finished components were taken to the main workshop to be dried out. There, curved sections such as the back and arm bows – made of yew – were steamed into the required shape by a 'bender'. A 'framer' then dowelled the assembled pieces into the 2 inch (5 cm) thick, traditionally saddle-shaped seats made from a single piece of well-seasoned elm. This wood neither warped, shrank nor split easily and was therefore extremely durable.

Because the chairs were composed of several woods, each chosen for specific qualities of durability or flexibility, many chairs were painted green, or japanned black to give them a uniform finish. Others were simply sand-scoured.

### 18TH-CENTURY DESIGNS

From about 1720, Windsor chairs had a comb-back design. Taper-turned 'sticks' formed a tall, straight back section topped by a simple crest rail. The sticks were

▼ The shape and proportions of the Windsor chair sometimes attracted more 'serious' craftsmen. This Regency version of a comb-back is made in mahogany, and exploits to the full that wood's ability to take intricate carving.

▼ Gothic Windsors first appeared in the 1760s. They were so called because their backs were pointed arches and the open fretwork splats were reminiscent of tracery. This one has cabriole legs, crinoline stretcher and a deep-cut seat.

# Wheel-back Windsor

FLAT CENTRAL SPLATS WERE ADDED TO WINDSOR CHAIRS FROM THE LAST QUARTER OF THE 18TH CENTURY. THEY WERE USUALLY DECORATED WITH FRETWORK DESIGNS. THE SIX-SPOKED WHEEL WAS A POPULAR MOTIF FROM THE BEGINNING — THIS EXAMPLE DATES FROM AROUND 1780 — AND HAS GIVEN ITS NAME TO A STYLE OF CHAIR. THE BACK SPINDLES ON EITHER SIDE OF THE SPLAT CONTINUE THROUGH THE ARM BOW INTO THE SEAT, WHILE THE ARM BOW SPLAYS OUT FOR EXTRA COMFORT.

UNUSUALLY, THIS CHAIR IS MADE ENTIRELY OF YEW-WOOD, INCLUDING THE SADDLE SEAT, AND THIS HAS WORN TO A FINE, RICH, WARM PATINA. THE SIMPLE TURNED LEGS ARE DOWELLED RIGHT THROUGH THE SEAT, AND ARE STRENGTHENED BY THE CURVED STRETCHER KNOWN AS A CRINOLINE OR COW-HORN. THE BACK LEGS ARE SPLAYED BACK AND OUT FOR GREATER RIGIDITY.

1. SPLAT CARVED WITH WHEEL MOTIF.

2. SPLAYED ARM BOW.

3. LEGS DOWELLED THROUGH SEAT.

4. WELL-WORN SADDLE SEAT.

5. CURVED CRINOLINE STRETCHER.

## Mendlesham Chair

MENDLESHAM CHAIRS, WITH THEIR DISTINCTIVE DOUBLE RAIL BACKS, WERE MADE IN EAST ANGLIA. THIS PLUMWOOD CHAIR IS FROM DISS, NORFOLK.

In the late 18th century and continuing into the early 19th century, the vase or urn-shaped splat was introduced. Then, from 1810-1820, when 'Prinny' became Prince Regent during the decline of George III, the Prince of Wales' feathers became a popular design motif on the splat.

The smoker's bow variant of the Windsor chair also came into fashion at this time. A solid, squat design, it had a lower back than its predecessors and thicker bobbin-turned sticks. The back hoop into which these

were fixed was surmounted by a curved crest. The legs were bulbous and the stretchers usually H-shaped.

### DISTINCTIVE STYLES

One of the most distinctive early 19th-century styles was the Mendlesham Windsor, which originated in the village of Mendlesham, Suffolk, another major chair-making centre. This design lacked the back splat and sticks stretching from the top rail right down to the seat; instead, it had a top and cross rail making a rectangular back

frame which contained a short, decorative central splat flanked by several slender spindles. Both rails consisted of two parallel bars joined by small wooden balls; the lower of the bottom pair curved down slightly towards the seat. This extremely elegant design was not produced on a large scale and is very rare today.

Another design with a 'free' lower back was the scroll-back Windsor. This side chair had two slightly backward-curving stiles ending in scrolls, with two back rails fixed between them.

# ·PRICE GUIDE· ⟩ *Windsor Chairs*

▲ A VERY PLAIN WELSH COUNTRY CHAIR OF THE 1820S. THE THICK ELM SEAT HAS NO SADDLE AND THERE ARE NO STRETCHERS.

PRICE GUIDE ❻

▲ A WELL-WORN, PAINTED WELSH COMB-BACK CHAIR OF 1780 WITH SHORT SPLAYED LEGS AND A SOLID CHESTNUT SEAT.

PRICE GUIDE ❼

▲ THE LOWER HALF OF THIS REGENCY CHAIR IS LIKE A SMOKER'S BOW. THE SPLAT CUT WITH HEARTS TIES IT TO A MORE CONVENTIONAL TOP.

PRICE GUIDE ❽

▲ THIS REGENCY SIDE-CHAIR IN ELM AND ASH HAS A BACK SUPPORTED BY A BRACE AND BOBTAIL AND THE PRINCE OF WALES' FEATHERS ON THE SPLAT.

PRICE GUIDE ❼

▶ AN EARLY 20TH CENTURY VERSION OF THE WHEELBACK. IT LACKS THE CONTINUOUS HOOP-BACK AND THE PATINA OF EARLIER CHAIRS.

PRICE GUIDE ❹

◀ A TYPICAL VERSION OF THE WINDSOR CHAIR FROM THE VERY EARLY VICTORIAN PERIOD. THE LEGS ARE NOT DOWELLED RIGHT THROUGH THE ELM SEAT.

PRICE GUIDE ❻

The plain upper rail was 4 to 6 inches (10 to 15 cm) deep, the lower one about half that depth and often decorative, as in the Nelson Windsor. This scroll-back style with twist turning on the lower scroll rail was made from about 1810 to 1840, commemorating Nelson's death at Trafalgar in 1805.

Another distinctive style, introduced in about 1810 and popular until the 1870s, was the Interlaced Bow Windsor. Instead of spindles or splats, this had a curved back frame containing interlaced wooden bands, arched in Gothic style.

The Windsor chair was also made in America from the 1720s. There, too, many designs evolved – but in different woods. Tulip-wood, poplar and pine were used for the seats, and chestnut, oak and hickory for the bent elements (such as backs and arm bows) and for the turned parts; the latter were also made of maple.

The 18th-century American Windsor chairs had higher backs than those of British design, and were usually entirely made up of spindles. Also, the seats were thicker, with the 'saddle' more pronounced, and the rather splayed legs were set in from the edges of the seat.

A typically American design of the late 18th and early 19th century was the arrow-back, whose flattened back spindles were carved into downward-pointing arrows.

Several of the most popular American low-back Windsor designs – including the Captain's chair, which was first used on Mississippi steamboats – were adopted in Britain in the early 19th century.

## POINTS TO WATCH

■ Graining should be clearly evident on both top and underside of the seat, as timber was always split, not sawn. Beware of saw marks.

■ There should be plain, taper-turned tenon joints and no nails.

■ Legs of beech, birch or fruitwood were prone to worm and wear and may have been replaced. Suspect this if the legs are of elm, matching the seat.

■ Sets of chairs should be identical in every respect, including seat and back heights.

# Cooking Utensils

The wooden, pottery and metal utentils that were
essential equipment for the cook in Regency England,
are now collectable items that can make a highly
effective display in the modern kitchen

The neat rows of copper pans, earthenware bowls and wooden ladles that were displayed in the Regency kitchen all played an essential role in the endless round of preserving, boiling and baking, roasting and toasting. Most of these culinary activities were carried out in time-honoured ways with utensils that had hardly changed for centuries, but others were made easier by the evolution of new pots and pans to suit the new method of cooking on a range, which was far cleaner, safer and more convenient than cooking on an open fire.

### THE KITCHEN RANGE
During the early years of the 18th century, coal replaced wood as the household fuel, and enclosed kitchen ranges gradually took over from hearths with open fires. Methods of roasting and boiling – and the utensils involved – changed accordingly. But this change was neither overnight nor universal. While modern-looking kettles and flat-bottomed pots simmered on ranges in the kitchens of large town houses, the heavy three-footed cauldron or kettle hanging in the chimney would have been a more usual sight in the country cottage of a remote area.

▶ *Although antique kitchenware is usually collected for its historical interest, the sturdier items such as wooden boards and bowls still have a practical use.*

In the advanced Georgian kitchen, cast-iron roasting equipment such as spits, grid irons and tall free-standing tripod toasters were still based on ancient designs but were now specifically adapted for use with the enclosed kitchen range. Larger joints of meat were roasted on a spit that hooked directly on to the grate, or were suspended vertically on a dangle-spit. Smaller spits were designed for birds, and basket spits were made to contain fish and meats which

fragmented during cooking. Smaller cuts of meat were grilled on a grid-iron, a four-footed iron grid with a drip tray and a long handle, which rested on the grate. Pieces of meat could also be impaled on the spikes of a free-standing iron toaster with tripod base which was placed in front of the fire. Bread, muffins, bacon, kippers and cheese could be toasted on the end of hand-held, three-pronged toasting forks made of iron, steel or brass.

## Early Cauldron

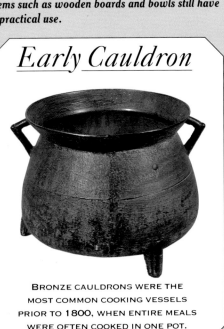

BRONZE CAULDRONS WERE THE
MOST COMMON COOKING VESSELS
PRIOR TO 1800, WHEN ENTIRE MEALS
WERE OFTEN COOKED IN ONE POT.

As it sizzled on the spit, meat was basted with a long-handled basting spoon, usually made of brass. By Georgian times, continuous turning to ensure even cooking was done mechanically by a device known as a spit-jack. A clockwork weight-driven spit-jack was in use as early as 1600, but by the 18th century, the bottle-jack and smoke-jack were the usual mechanical devices for turning the spit. The smoke-jack was a combination of wheels and chains which, linked to the spit, was driven by a fan activated by hot air currents in the throat of the chimney. The bottle-jack, so called because of its shape, was a spring-driven device that hung from the chimney breast and rotated on a vertical axis, leaving the area in front of the fire free.

Potatoes and salted meats such as hams were boiled in large oval cast-iron pots. These flat-bottomed vessels were specially designed for the hobs and hotplates that

▲ *An early 19th-century print of a farmhouse kitchen showing the various utensils used to make the oatcakes that are cooking on the bakestone – a large earthenware bowl and ladle for mixing batter, and a wooden riddle board. Finished oatcakes are hung from the ceiling on a creel.*

▶ *Rows of gleaming copper utensils line the walls of the kitchen at Saltram House. On the well-scrubbed table sit skillets, cones and jugs, and above them are the pots and pans.*

were soon added to kitchen ranges, and they must have looked conspicuously modern by comparison with the earlier round-bottomed cauldrons and skillets on tripod feet. Flat-bottomed copper kettles placed on the hob heated water. For kitchen ranges without a hob, pots with handles could still be suspended in the chimney in the old-fashioned way. Sauces were heated in small pans placed on trivets that hooked on to the bars of the grate.

## IRON OVENS

From the mid-18th century, new iron ovens provided better temperature control for baking. Bread and oatcakes were placed in the oven on bakestones, and for pies there were oval dishes made of tin-plate or earthenware.

In Georgian and Regency kitchens, roasting, boiling and baking were only half the culinary story. The dinner table was laden with attractive displays of meat, pies, puddings and cold sweets, the preparation of which involved an immense amount of chopping and mixing, pounding and beating. For this, there were wooden spoons, boards and bowls, steel knives and a whole range of small utensils.

## THE KITCHEN DRESSER

Many of these smaller utensils were kept in the drawers or on the shelves of the large kitchen dresser. On this important piece of kitchen furniture rested rows of jelly moulds, plates and bowls, with hand-held implements such as spoons and ladles neatly hanging on the hooks.

# Wooden and Pottery Kitchenware

Many of the wooden and pottery items found in the Regency kitchen were used for baking, preparing vegetables and making sauces.

Flour and yeast were mixed in bowls carved from a single piece of wood, and the dough was kneaded, cut and shaped on large wooden boards before being placed in the oven in an earthenware bread crock. Pastry was rolled and cut with a wooden rolling pin and pastry cutters. Attractively carved wooden moulds impressed patterns on to cakes and gingerbread and pats of butter, and miniature wooden chests of drawers held fragrant spices.

Wood, generally ash, elm or beech, was also used to make

spinach pressers, lemon squeezers, potato mashers and meat and fish hammers, while hard lignum vitae was the preferred material for coffee mills.

Earthenware was equally important in the kitchen. The earthenware pestle and mortar was essential for pulverizing and mixing spices, breadcrumbs and other ingredients for sauces, flavourings and colourings. The well-equipped kitchen would have had three or four in different sizes.

Finally, there were slip-glazed earthenware salt jars and shallow pie dishes, stoneware and earthenware moulds for mousses and creams, and an array of pottery jugs and small bowls for spices and sauces.

*A well-worn wooden two-handled bread board or platter dating from around 1790.*

PRICE GUIDE **5**

▲ *A late-Georgian earthenware dish with slip decoration. Slipware was traditionally made by country potters.*

PRICE GUIDE **4**

◄ *A concave wooden chopping board with its chopper, dating from c.1800.*

PRICE GUIDE **6**

▶ *A butter curler from c.1800 with charmingly naive decoration.*

PRICE GUIDE **3**

▲ *An early 19th-century wood and steel slicer for cheese or vegetables, with guillotine action.*

PRICE GUIDE **3**

PRICE GUIDE

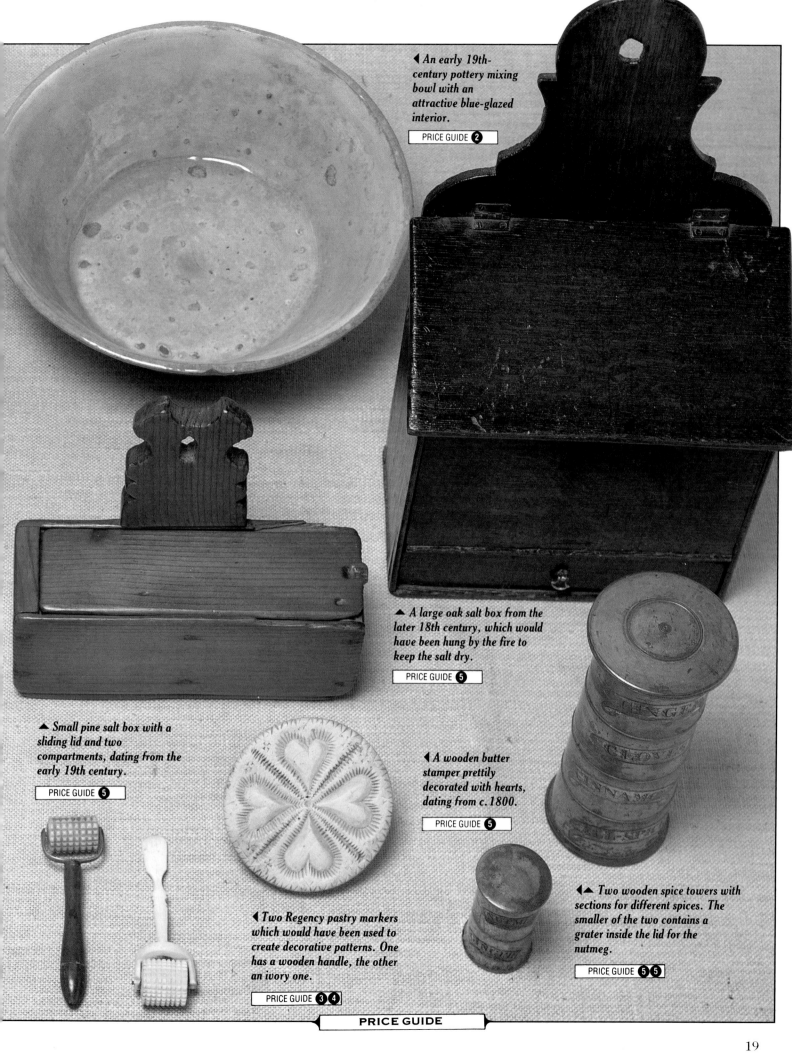

◀ An early 19th-century pottery mixing bowl with an attractive blue-glazed interior.

PRICE GUIDE ❷

▲ A large oak salt box from the later 18th century, which would have been hung by the fire to keep the salt dry.

PRICE GUIDE ❺

▲ Small pine salt box with a sliding lid and two compartments, dating from the early 19th century.

PRICE GUIDE ❺

◀ A wooden butter stamper prettily decorated with hearts, dating from c. 1800.

PRICE GUIDE ❺

◀▲ Two wooden spice towers with sections for different spices. The smaller of the two contains a grater inside the lid for the nutmeg.

PRICE GUIDE ❺❺

◀ Two Regency pastry markers which would have been used to create decorative patterns. One has a wooden handle, the other an ivory one.

PRICE GUIDE ❸❹

**PRICE GUIDE**

# Metal Utensils

The Regency kitchen boasted an impressive array of iron, tin-plate, copper and brass equipment. Besides the great iron pots and heavy frying pans, there were copper or brass pans and kettles, iron griddles and waffle irons. Other cooking implements included iron flesh forks, toasting forks and large-bowled, long-handled brass basting spoons with a pierced handle for hanging. Smoke-jacks and bottle-jacks to turn the spit were virtually the only mechanical devices that lightened the heavy work load.

Cutting was done with steel knives of various sizes, and chopping with square or semi-circular iron choppers with wooden handles. Graters, dredgers, fish slices, tin-plate pie dishes, pastry cutters and metal colanders, some of which were also made in wood or earthenware, were equally important utensils.

▶ Late-Georgian coffee pot. The wooden handle is attached to the pot with a heart-shaped plate.

PRICE GUIDE ❺

▶ Small copper saucepan with lid, dating from around 1790. Like most copper pans, this one is tinned inside to prevent poisons in the copper contaminating the food.

PRICE GUIDE ❺

▶ A small meat cleaver made of steel and wood from the late 18th century.

PRICE GUIDE ❹

▲ This oddly-shaped steel and wood implement was used for chopping parsley. It was made in about 1800.

PRICE GUIDE ❺

▶ A cruciform wooden pastry jigger with two stamps on the side arms for marking biscuits.

PRICE GUIDE ❺

◀ An unusually attractive steel kitchen chopper from c.1800, used for vegetables and meat.

PRICE GUIDE ❺

▲ Adjustable brass and steel pincers from c.1780, used for suspending meat over the fire.

PRICE GUIDE ❺

**PRICE GUIDE**

► *Two tin-plate ale mullers, one conical and one slipper-shaped, both dating from c.1800. They were used to warm home-brewed beer in the fire.*

PRICE GUIDE **5** **3**

▼ *Brass and steel skimmer from the Regency period, for skimming the fat from milk and sauces.*

PRICE GUIDE **5**

▲ *Brass ladle with a steel handle, dating from c.1800.*

PRICE GUIDE **5**

▲ *Steel and wood toasting fork c.1790, used for holding muffins, bread or kippers in front of the fire.*

PRICE GUIDE **4**

▲ *Late 18th-century heavy brass pestle and mortar, which would have pulverized herbs and spices.*

PRICE GUIDE **4**

PRICE GUIDE

## COLLECTOR'S TIPS

At the time they were made and used, basic cooking utensils were generally regarded as functional implements with little intrinsic value. In any case, continuous chopping, stirring, roasting and boiling took their toll. Earthenware chipped and broke, and wooden bowls and spoons cracked or disintegrated. Metal implements, when they snapped, sprang a leak or lost a leg or prong, were discarded or consigned to the melting pot. By the end of the 19th century, the advent of stoves and cookers had made many of them redundant, and it is only in comparatively recent times that ordinary, functional and humble cooking utensils have been salvaged and collected for their historical interest. Regency cooking utensils are consequently rarer than many other objects dating from that era.

### DURABLE METAL UTENSILS

Metal utensils have survived in the greatest numbers as they are the most durable. Iron or brass trivets, for example, are among the most frequently seen relics of cooking at the hearth or range. Free-standing trivets are slightly more common than those with wooden handles and frontal hooks for fixing to the grate. Iron trivets generally, though by no means always, predate brass trivets, though this does not make them more valuable.

Many toasting forks have also survived and it is the more decorative brass toasting forks that are most commonly found today although rarer plain iron or steel steak forks and toasters are as highly prized.

Heavy metal sugar and herb choppers are also quite frequently encountered, but knives, metal strainers, skimmers and colanders are harder to come by. Bottle-jacks, which were usually discarded as they wore out, are now rarities.

Of the Georgian and Regency wooden and earthenware cooking utensils, small wooden ladles, scoops, spoons and pastry jiggers can be picked up the most cheaply. Wooden pestles and mortars occupy the

### COMPARISONS

## Saucepan Styles

MANY REGENCY KITCHENS HAD A KITCHEN RANGE THAT COMBINED AN OPEN FIRE WITH A HOB. THE BRASS CAULDRON ON THE LEFT WOULD HAVE HUNG OVER THE FIRE, WHILE THE COPPER SAUCEPAN ON THE RIGHT WOULD HAVE SAT ON THE HOB.

## The Coffee Grinder

IN REGENCY BRITAIN, COFFEE WAS STILL A LUXURY DRINK, AND THE UTENSILS ASSOCIATED WITH IT WERE OFTEN ACCORDED A SPECIAL STATUS. THIS BEAUTIFULLY TURNED LIGNUM VITAE COFFEE GRINDER IS TYPICAL OF MANY FINE 18TH- AND 19TH-CENTURY EXAMPLES. IT INCORPORATES A CONICAL CUTTER WHICH IS TURNED BY A DETACHABLE CRANK HANDLE. WHEN NOT IN USE, THE HANDLE CAN BE FOLDED UP AND STORED INSIDE THE BODY OF THE MILL, AND THE WOODEN LID SCREWED ON IN ITS PLACE. BECAUSE THEY WERE PRESTIGIOUS OBJECTS, COFFEE MILLS WERE OFTEN KEPT IN THE PARLOUR RATHER THAN THE KITCHEN.

① THE DETACHABLE HANDLE CAN BE STOWED AWAY WHEN NOT IN USE.

② THE THREE SECTIONS CAN BE PULLED APART TO REVEAL THE GRINDING MECHANISM IN THE MIDDLE AND THE GROUND COFFEE IN THE BOTTOM.

③ LIGNUM VITAE IS A TROPICAL HARDWOOD WITH A DENSE GRAIN, MAKING IT HIGHLY SU!TABLE FOR SMALL CARVED OR TURNED OBJECTS.

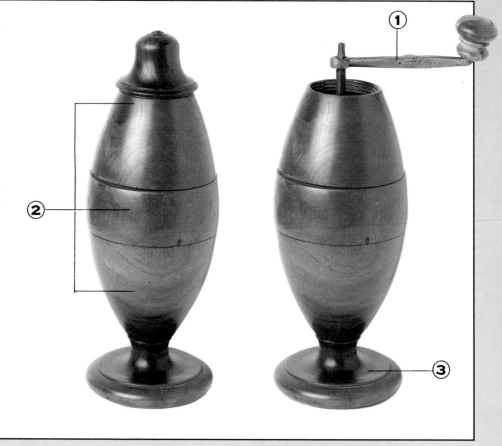

·CLOSE UP·

① INCISED DECORATION

② SLIPWARE

③ BISCUIT STAMPER

④ CERAMIC FLOWER

① THE HANDLE OF THE BUTTER CURLER HAS A SIMPLE INCISED PATTERN

② SLIP – CLAY MIXED WITH WATER – WAS OFTEN USED TO DECORATE RUSTIC EARTHENWARE

③ THE SIDE ARMS OF THE PASTRY JIGGER MARK PATTERNS ON BISCUITS

④ THE UNDERSIDE OF THE EARTHENWARE BOWL IS DECORATED WITH A FLOWER

⑤ EVEN THE HANDLE OF THE BUTTER STAMPER BEARS AN ATTRACTIVE DESIGN

⑤ CARVED HANDLE

middle price range, while large wooden bowls are rarer and therefore more highly priced. As they are now fashionable collectables, wooden butter pats and gingerbread moulds are no longer cheap. Rarity also makes the wooden coffee grinder one of the more expensive pieces of Georgian kitchen equipment. A good oak and brass-mounted coffee grinder will, however, command less than half the price of a fine lignum vitae example.

### DATING A PIECE

It is seldom possible to date Georgian or Regency cooking equipment accurately. An actual date of manufacture or maker's mark is almost unknown on cooking utensils made before the Victorian era.

However, there are some general guides to dating. In the case of trivets and toasting forks, for example, the more elaborate the decoration, the more recent the manufacture. A plain iron trivet or toasting fork is likely to predate a more ornate brass one. Plain, lidded, flat-bottomed cooking pots are likely to date from between the late 18th and mid-19th centuries. Those bearing a maker's mark or plaque are likely to be Victorian or later. Enamelled iron pots are also likely to be Victorian. As they

remained virtually unchanged for many decades, wooden and earthenware utensils are difficult to date.

Rust spots and stains can be removed from iron or steel utensils by gentle rubbing with fine sand paper or steel wool, but care should be taken not to rub harshly over decorative details.

Surface dirt and tarnish on brass or copper is best removed by soapy water. Engrained dirt can then be polished away with a metal polish. The wooden handles of basting spoons, toasting forks and handled trivets can be revived with wax polish. Wooden bowls, spoons and other wooden utensils need little attention other than an occasional light coating of cooking oil to prevent the wood from drying out.

### POINTS TO WATCH

■ Fine metal implements, particularly in brass, are often faked. Genuine pieces should have convincing signs of wear.

■ Although plain iron utensils, wooden bowls, spoons and other small pieces are likely to be genuine, it is worth checking for

▶ *A sturdy pair of spit dogs support two spits, which can be moved up or down to suit different roasting requirements.*

authentic evidence of wear and unevenness.

■ Dating being difficult, collectors should bear in mind that some utensils in use in the 18th century were also made up until the late 19th century.

■ Unless a piece is rare, condition is important; damaged kitchen utensils can be difficult to repair.

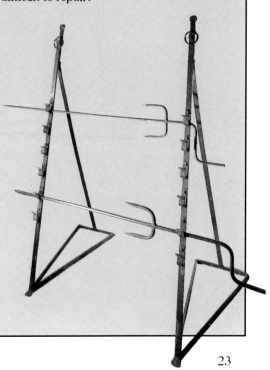

# The Jelly Mould

Jelly moulds, in a range of materials such as earthenware, copper and glass, played a vital role in the Regency kitchen, where they were used to make spectacular displays for the dining table

The upper classes of the Regency period dined in conscious splendour. As well as a superb range of glass and silver vessels and utensils, their tables were decorated with exquisite porcelain figures and crowned with large, elaborate centrepieces of opulent silver or such spectacularly impermanent materials as wax, sugar and ice.

## AN EDIBLE DISPLAY

The dessert course offered the perfect opportunity for additional display, since it was often served separately in the drawing room, or even featured as a meal in its own right at the informal parties known as 'routs', so popular among the Regency fast set. 'Dressing out the dessert' was one of the accomplishments of the complete hostess, under whose direction the assorted puddings in fanciful shapes were laid out alongside arrangements of fruit, nuts and comfits.

▼ *Although today's jelly moulds are rather uninspired by comparison, those made in centuries past were prized for their decorative qualities even when not in use. In the mid-18th century most jelly moulds were very small and were designed to serve only one person. By the Regency period, however, they had become large enough for multiple servings.*

But most impressive of all were the glittering pyramids of salvers, each salver holding a colourful array of glasses containing jellies, blancmanges, syllabubs and similar edible delights.

For its unseen creators – the cook and his helpers – all this meant a great deal of hard work and a huge expenditure of time. The making of a jelly might be spread over 24 hours and involved a host of laborious tasks such as boning, boiling, straining, skimming, and whipping, some of which were repeated more than once.

Although there were all too few labour-saving devices available, the mould was a prized piece of equipment, and the grander Regency kitchen would have had scores of them, intended for all sorts of edibles. The wide variety of moulds devised solely for jellies reflected the decorative properties of this dessert, for jellies could be made in a range of colours and lent themselves to the creation of stable, crisply detailed 'sculptures'.

The basic ingredient of jelly was gelatine, made from sheeps' heads, cows' feet or deer antlers (used to make hartshorn jelly). In Britain, meat jellies or aspics were known as early as the 14th century, and in 1509 the jellies at a royal banquet 'surpassed everything, being made in the shape of castles and animals of various descriptions, as beautiful and as admirable as can be imagined'.

Although these imaginatively-shaped jellies were probably made with moulds, none of these have survived. The earliest known moulds date from around 1730 and were the work of Staffordshire

▲ *Jellies were known to be a popular dessert at banquets as early as 1466, when a great feast for the Archbishop of York took place. At banquets in the 18th century, the table was laid with tiers of glass salvers filled with glasses of jelly, cream and sweetmeats, their arrangement on the table strictly following the guidelines set by professional confectioners.*

potters. By this time, sugar from the West Indies was widely available and jelly had become popular as a sweet as well as a savoury dish.

The introduction of isinglass (a form of gelatine made from fish) as a setting agent improved the jelly's appearance, which was further enhanced by a variety of natural colourings. Cochineal was used for red, spinach for green, saffron for yellow, syrup of violets for blue, chocolate for brown and thick cream for white. A range of flavourings, made from fruit, nuts and wines, ensured that the dessert jelly was every bit as delicious as it looked.

### STARS AND STRIPES

Not surprisingly, there was a substantial demand for jelly moulds in middle- and upper-class kitchens, and a wide range was available in terms of both quality and elaboration. Then as now, ridged, ribbed and twisted designs were popular, as were relicfs of moons, stars, suns, shells and other simple shapes on the bases of moulds. More sophisticated designs included birds, flowers, melons and the ever-popular pineapple, which the Georgians seem to have found especially appealing.

Many early moulds were made from the white salt-glazed stoneware produced by Staffordshire potters, a sturdy and reliable ware with an interesting granular surface. The most popular of all the stoneware moulds were fish-shaped, probably because they were so easy to arrange into simple but effective scenes. One great recipe book favourite was to lay a fish moulded from an opaque substance –

usually blancmange or flummery – in a 'pool' of clear jelly, which rippled satisfyingly at the slightest touch.

Flummery and blancmange were closely related to jelly and were often used with it in decorative displays. Flummery was an old established favourite, made from hartshorn jelly thickened with oatmeal, and blancmange was a kind of meat jelly for most of the Regency period, only acquiring its separate present-day character as a dessert in the 1820s, when arrowroot was imported as a thickener which could be mixed with boiling sweetened milk.

### WEDGWOOD MOULDS

In the later 18th century, salt-glazed stoneware met with fierce competition from earthenware products, and in particular from the new, smooth-bodied, highly fashionable creamwares and pearlwares. Among the pioneers of this trend were Josiah Wedgwood's famous firm and rivals and imitators such as the Spode and Leeds factories.

Many jelly and other moulds were manufactured in these new materials, and Wedgwood's cool neo-classicism is apparent in examples with antique gem designs, Egyptian symbols and phoenixes. A large amount of creamware was produced for middle-class consumers with relatively plain tastes. Wedgwood moulds were of an elegant simplicity and often came as 'nests' – moulds, identical in shape but of different sizes, that fitted neatly into one another.

## Decorative Styles

TYPICALLY-SHAPED COPPER JELLY MOULD WITH TIN LINING WHICH SAFEGUARDED AGAINST VERDIGRIS POISONING.

A CREAMWARE JELLY MOULD WITH GRAPE DESIGN RESTING ON AN EARLY FORM OF PEG FEET, FROM c.1820.

At the other extreme were the Wedgwood two-part or core moulds, which were used to create sumptuous display pieces. As well as the usual outer mould, this came with a 'core' that fitted into it, leaving very little space to spare. The core was an elegant object, shaped like a cone, wedge or pyramidal pillar, and usually more or less reminiscent of the columns and obelisks of antiquity which the Georgians so admired. They were also delicately painted in bright enamel colours with a variety of flowers and plants.

The core was inserted into the mould after the jelly had been poured in. When it had set, the mould was removed and the core remained, covered with a thin, even layer of jelly. This made an interesting visual display for the table since the decoration of the core was magnified by the jelly.

These jellies were, of course, purely showpieces, and as such not intended for consumption, but their decorative charm was considerable, especially when the core also had novelty value. In 1782 Parson Woodforde, a Suffolk clergyman, noted in his diary that he had dined at a house where the table boasted 'a very pretty Pyramid of Jelly in the centre, a landscape appearing thro' the Jelly, a new device and brought from London'.

Moulds with rounded or irregular bases (representing the tops of turned-out jellies) were difficult to keep upright while they set. One solution to the problem was to stabilize the base by means of thin, inconspicuous pegs. However, these proved too fragile to survive the hurly-burly of a large kitchen, and it subsequently became quite common to make

## ·PRICE GUIDE· ▷ PUDDING UTENSILS

*Perhaps the most collectable of all moulds are those made in stoneware and creamware, since many people collect these alone. Copper moulds are less valuable, although they are sometimes preferred for their striking appearance on a kitchen shelf.*

▲ *Although lead is the best insulator for keeping food cold, it was known to cause lead poisoning, and moulds were made from pewter with only a small amount of lead.*

▲▷ *Although jellies were stiff enough in the Regency period to be turned out of moulds, they were still served in glasses and cut-glass serving dishes.*

PRICE GUIDE **5**

▲ *Pewter ice-cream mould with tight-fitting lid which would have been placed in ice to freeze.*

PRICE GUIDE **4**

▼ *Simple wooden lemon squeezer dating from c.1800.*

PRICE GUIDE **4**

◀ *Individual-sized copper moulds, which probably were purchased as part of a set of varying sizes.*

PRICE GUIDE **3**

moulds with substantial rims attached to their bases. This rather spoiled the appearance of a mould, but as they were not seen outside the kitchen, this was not considered important.

Many of the more elaborate moulds continued to be stabilized by traditional methods. This meant bedding them in sand (always to hand in the kitchen, since it was used as a scouring agent) or, if the setting had to be done at short notice, in ice. Such an operation could be tricky in the case of a really elaborate structure such as 'Solomon's Temple', featured in *The Experienced English Housekeeper* of 1769, with its four corner turrets and high obelisk-like central tower.

To make the cook's task still harder, such showpieces were expected to be multi-coloured. This multi-coloured 'ribbon jelly' was popular and prestigious almost throughout the Georgian era, since the arrangement of adjacent but distinct, unblurred colours created a pleasing rainbow effect while demonstrating the skill and devotion of the kitchen staff. Great care was needed in making it, for, as a recipe book noted, 'one colour must be thorough cold before you put another on, and that you run on must not be blood-warm for fear it mixes together'.

Although ceramic moulds remained in use and pressed glass was introduced during the 19th century, from late Regency times copper was the most fashionable material. In well-to-do households the vogue for jelly and blancmange desserts – both for display and for consumption – continued throughout the Victorian period and into the Edwardian era.

## Regency Puddings

For dessert, the sweet-toothed Regency diner was confronted with an enviably wide range of puddings. As well as jellies and blancmanges, the fare might include curds and creams, flummeries and syllabubs, ice cream, sorbets and preserved fruits. Immense labour was expended on preparing these in the kitchen. The relatively simple recipe for calves' foot jelly in Mrs Smith's *Compleat Housewife* involved boiling down 4 calves' feet in water, sieving the result, letting it cool, boiling it with wine, lemon and sugar and the whites of eight eggs beaten to a froth, before it was sieved continuously until it was 'clear as water'.

▼▶ In order to prepare such a wide range of puddings the Regency cook would refer to a recipe book such as *The Compleat Confectioner*.

◀ **Curd mould in Leeds creamware, the interior decorated with a fish, dating from c.1820.**

PRICE GUIDE **6**

▶ **Copper moulds really became popular at the end of the Regency era when the majority were produced in Birmingham and the Midlands.**

PRICE GUIDE **5**

▼ **Creamware moulds showing corn and flowers, one for an individual serving, one for a family.**

PRICE GUIDE **4**

◀ **Small bone spoons dating from c.1820, which would have been used to eat delicacies like jelly or flummery.**

PRICE GUIDE **3**

# The Nutmeg Grater

Once a treasured possession that enabled the owner to
have a supply of freshly grated nutmeg on hand, the
Georgian nutmeg grater can still be found in silver, wood
and ivory

The Georgian nutmeg grater was likely to be made in silver, and was designed to be carried in the pocket. It was an increasingly fashionable accoutrement used both in the tavern and at the dining table to season food and drink with the freshly ground spice.

The nutmeg first came to Europe at the time of the Crusades. In the 14th century Chaucer mentioned 'notemuge to put in ale', but the spice was not regularly imported into Europe until the Portuguese captured the spice trade in the early 16th century. Magellan's celebrated circumnavigation of the globe, completed in 1522, was inspired not by gold or silver but by the search for a western route to the Moluccas and their valuable produce – cloves and nutmeg.

During the Georgian period nutmegs were in great demand for their flavour and medicinal properties and were imported under the auspices of the English East India Company. Directorial meetings were cheered by a brandy punch recipe ending with the suggestion 'and if you please, one nutmeg grated.'

## A TOUCH OF SPICE

The nutmeg was also used for the flavouring of hot possets, caudle (a warm drink given to the sick), negus (mulled wine) and hot toddy. A dietary of

*◀ Although nutmeg is today relegated to the kitchen to flavour the odd dish, it was prized by the Georgians who carried their own supply and used it for almost everything – from spicing ale, hot drinks and food and even for soothing a cold.*

1542 claims that 'nutmeges be good for them the whiche have colde in theyr hed', and by the 18th century they were generally regarded as a panacea. Such beverages were also probably imbibed with an eye to the nutmeg's reputed hallucinogenic and aphrodisiac properties.

Numerous savoury dishes, such as Hannah Glasse's celebrated recipe for roast hare, as well as sweet ones such as custards, marchpane (marzipan) and 'minc'd pyes', benefited from a sprinkling of nutmeg. One delightful recipe from Elizabeth Raffald's *Experienced English House-Keeper* (1771), entitled 'How to make Syllabub under the Cow', required a bottle of strong beer, a pint of cider, sugar, a small nutmeg and 'as much milk from the cow as will make a strong froth'.

## EARLY NUTMEG GRATERS

Nutmeg graters were made from bone, brass, pewter, ivory, wood and tin, but more commonly from silver and silver plate. It seems possible that the first examples were originally made of silver and were incorporated in the travelling canteens which became popular in the late 17th century. The more elaborate varieties would consist of a tumbler into which would fit a spoon, fork, knife, spice box, napkin hook, corkscrew, apple-corer and nutmeg grater, all contained in a shagreen leather case.

The earliest silver nutmeg graters were uniformly

*Myristica or Nutmeg Tree.*

▲ *Highly spiced food was the fashion as early as Elizabethan times and wealthier households bought their spices from local small-town dealers whose stock included gilded nutmegs. In Georgian kitchens, where much time and energy went into preparing basic ingredients for the popular spicy cooking, a nutmeg grater was one of a wide range of kitchen implements indispensable to the cook. Kitchen graters were generally made from base metal, unlike the more elaborate silver pocket graters carried around by the members of the household.*

cylindrical and date from about 1670, continuing through to around 1730. Usually between 2.5 and 3 inches (6.5-7.5cm) long and up to 1 inch (2.5cm) in diameter, they consist of a cylindrical silver grater or rasp, a circular pull-off cap and a cylindrical case. Occasionally a section is reserved for the nutmeg, involving a second cap at the other end. The case is often engraved, usually with simple geometric motifs on the sides and perhaps a tulip (possibly a reference to the Dutch control of the spice trade) or a star shape on the lid. If present, the hallmark is located on the rim. Some examples are pierced and possibly acted as pomanders since evidence of other spices has been detected.

From the late 17th to well into the 18th century the teardrop or heart-shaped nutmeg grater became *de rigueur*. These were possibly given as love tokens, and had pull-off box-style lids which were later replaced by a three-lug hinge top and bottom, also used for circular, oval, square and rectangular boxes. One end opened out to reveal the grater, the other gave access to the nutmeg. Again, design motifs were quite simplistic, echoing those of the cylindrical models.

From 1739 to 1790 'Very small Nutmeg Graters' were decreed exempt from assaying. Rare indeed are examples of hallmarked nutmeg graters of this period. Identification has to rely on makers' marks. After this period the London Assay office punched

SILVER HEXAGONAL-SHAPED NUTMEG GRATER DELICATELY ENGRAVED WITH THE OWNER'S INITIAL IN THE CENTRE, C. 1800.

A JAPANNED OR ORIENTAL LACQUERED NUTMEG GRATER FINISHED WITH A SILVER EMBLEM ON THE LID.

DATING FROM C. 1800 THIS ACORN-SHAPED NUTMEG GRATER IS FINELY CARVED IN COQUILLA WOOD.

the complete hallmark inside the lid of the grater.

The rasp or grater section was originally made of silver, but freedom from assaying allowed the silversmiths to use hammered sheet steel and later rolled steel. This led to a problem with rust, despite tin or french plated coatings. The best solution was to harden the rolled steel sheeting in raw whale oil, thus creating a resistant hard blue film. Perforations on the grater were both handmade and factory done on a flypress.

### NOVELTY SHAPES

Novelty shapes proved popular. The egg-shaped grater, often associated with the London silversmith Samuel Massey, was popular in both bone and ivory. These unscrewed into two parts (though some later examples pull apart), the lower section being nearly twice the size of the upper, and were often beautifully chased or engraved with bright-cutting. Some even included a vinaigrette.

The so-called 'hydrant' type was closely akin to the oval variety. Both had pull-off interchangeable

·PRICE GUIDE· **GRATERS & GRINDERS**

*Nutmeg graters made from 1670-1840 are still available in a number of different styles. The majority are made in silver, although they may be found in Sheffield plate, brass, pewter, wood and ivory.*

▼ *A pestle and mortar was used for grinding whole spices such as cloves, cinnamon and pepper.*

PRICE GUIDE ❹

▼ *Rectangular silver nutmeg grater engraved with a checker-work design and a central phoenix crest, made by Joseph Willmore of Birmingham c.1800.*

PRICE GUIDE ❻

▼ *Silver pocket nutmeg grater dating from 1814, manufactured by Wardell & Kempson.*

PRICE GUIDE ❺

▼ *A more unusual nutmeg grater designed in black japanned metal.*

PRICE GUIDE ❹

*◀ The Georgians' demand for nutmeg was met by the English East India Company who imported spices, offloading them at London's appropriately named East India Wharf. Nutmeg as well as mace came from the Spice Islands (the Moluccas in Indonesia) and was the subject of feuds and intrigues among the European trading nations in the 17th and 18th centuries.*

lids, the upper section being domed to house the nutmeg. Many hydrant-shaped graters were made by Samuel Pemberton of Birmingham, active from 1773-1816, who specialized in small articles such as snuff and patch boxes and vinaigrettes.

Pemberton was also a prolific producer of acorn-shaped graters, which unscrewed into three sections. An embellishment of this style was the mace shape, the handle of which often concealed a corkscrew. This style was reputedly a pun on the word mace, the red outer layer of the nutmeg which was also used as a spice.

One of the most popular designs was the barrel shape, an allusion to the kegs of rum, whisky or brandy that were the prime constituent of hot toddy or punch. Wooden examples also survive, mostly made from coquilla wood which had been imported from the east coast of South Africa since the mid-16th century. This somewhat brittle but oily wood, which ranges from a deep brown to a tortoiseshell colour, was also used for richly carved graters in the shapes of acorns, bottles and shoes.

By the Regency period graters in a bucket shape made from sycamore had become popular. These were decorated with red and black lines or with handpainted or applied paper pictures on the lid with souvenir views such as the Royal Pavilion at Brighton.

The cylinder shape made a comeback during this period, but this time with a cutaway side panel to reveal the grater inside and with a hinged rather than pull-off lid. Hester Bateman produced several examples of this variety.

By the end of the Regency period lathe-turned work had gained a strong position in a market that was by now on the decline. Oblong reeded designs with a hinged lid and base were popular, as were novelty shapes based on natural forms such as snail shells, walnuts and fruits.

The larger 'kitchen' type nutmeg graters, ranging from 4 to 10 inches (10-25 cm) in length, made an appearance in the Regency period as accompaniments of the toddy bowl, in both the dining room and the tavern. These came in two styles, based on the traditional kitchen grater.

The sconce or semi-circular nutmeg grater had a silver backplate and looped handle embellished with gadrooning or cast shell and leaf motifs. With its design of concentric circles, the grater was occasionally protected by a sliding cover of silver or Sheffield plate. Both the base, which opened like the lid, and the backplate were fully hallmarked.

By the beginning of the 19th century tastes had changed, and nutmeg graters disappeared from use. Today they make charming collector's pieces, and many still carry a whiff of their spicy past!

*▼ Cylindrical nutmeg grater that pulls apart, with storage space for several nutmegs.*

PRICE GUIDE ❹

*▼ Herbs such as basil, marjoram, rosemary, parsley and thyme could be chopped with a sharp blade in this wooden bowl.*

PRICE GUIDE ❹

*▼ George III pocket nutmeg grater in silver made by John Linnit in 1819, with finely detailed decoration on all sides.*

PRICE GUIDE ❻

# Mason's Ironstone

Mason's Ironstone china comes in a wide range of designs and shapes, almost all of which are decorated in rich colours, making it extremely popular with collectors for its striking visual appeal

For today's collector, the appeal of Mason's Ironstone wares lies in their distinctively rich, bright colours and their pleasing, rather thick-set shapes. Across the range, from jugs and plates to vases and footbaths, Mason's Ironstone is robust yet colourful, with a rather homely feel to it. Allied to an affordable retail price, these were precisely the qualities that made Mason's Ironstone an instant success when it was launched in 1813.

Mason's Ironstone imitated the shapes and decoration of fine 18th-century porcelain. Although it was an earthenware, it effectively became the 'household china' of the aspiring middle classes who could not afford porcelain.

Mason's Ironstone is a strong, hardwearing stoneware pottery. It was developed in the early 19th century by Miles Mason, a porcelain dealer and manufacturer in the Staffordshire Potteries. Miles Mason's invention was patented by his son, Charles James Mason, in 1813; from then on the ware was known as 'Mason's Patent Ironstone China', and its manufacture over the following 35 years was to bring the family both fame and a considerable fortune.

### VIBRANT COLOURS

While Mason's Ironstone owed its success in no small part to the business acumen of Charles James Mason, it was his artistic brother, George Miles Mason, who developed the wares' distinctive decoration and rich palette of colours. The brothers traded as G. and C. Mason, and from the premises in Fenton which they named the Patent Ironstone Manufactory came an almost limitless range of domestic and decorative wares. These proved so successful that they were also exported to Canada and the United States.

Some years later, however, falling standards and labour troubles began to afflict the factory. By 1844, Charles James Mason was bankrupt and in 1848 the Patent Ironstone Manufactory was sold. However, many of the moulds and copper printing plates were acquired by one Francis Morley, who reinvigorated production and created new interest in the ware. The business was to change ownership twice more before becoming part of the Wedgwood group in 1973.

### METHOD OF MANUFACTURE

Mason's Patent Ironstone China was an ingenious name that conjured up both the strength of pottery and the refinement of porcelain. It was the name, as well as the colourful designs, that caught the public imagination. Far from being 'china', however, Mason's Ironstone was an earthenware pottery which gained its durability and hardness from a combination of raw materials which the patent of

*▼ Although it is associated with oriental patterns, Mason's Ironstone was produced in a wide range of designs. Collectors can choose either one particular style, or a range of different designs, both of which can produce an equally striking display.*

*▶ Brightly-coloured ewer and basin dating from c.1820 with a typically oriental floral design. The octagonal-shaped jug was a popular style and was often produced with these gilded, serpent-shaped handles.*

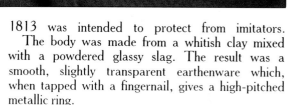

1813 was intended to protect from imitators.

The body was made from a whitish clay mixed with a powdered glassy slag. The result was a smooth, slightly transparent earthenware which, when tapped with a fingernail, gives a high-pitched metallic ring.

## TRANSFER PRINTING

In keeping with the economical, labour-saving methods of the day, the basic decoration on Mason's Ironstone was transfer-printed on to the body, which was then given a protective glaze. To produce the colourful polychrome decoration for which Mason's Ironstone is best known, artists at the Patent Ironstone Manufactory painted the transfer-printed design with coloured enamels. In this way, bright, almost luminous greens, blues and reds, together with subtler shaded washes, were applied. Gilding, also an integral part of much of the decoration on Mason's Ironstone, further embellished the rich enamel colours.

Designs took the form of all-over patterns on a white ground. Most were derived from the Japanese Imari pattern and other oriental designs including birds, butterflies and roses in full bloom.

Not all the patterns on Mason's Ironstone were derived from oriental designs, however. Decidedly European birds and flowers wreathed in rich gilding adorned many of Mason's European-style vases and ewers, and Italianate landscapes with classical ruins, again with rich gilding, were hand-painted on to the centre of plates and dishes.

During the early years of the Patent Ironstone

Manufactory – from 1813 up to about 1830 – standards of potting and decoration were high. By the 1830s, however, colours became harsher and the gilding less tastefully applied. The accurate imitation of Imari and other oriental patterns also degenerated.

During the 35 years of the factory's existence, Mason's produced an astonishingly wide range of wares. As well as individual pieces like teapots, mugs, bowls and covered dishes, there were extensive dinner and dessert services, and of course Mason's famous octagonal jugs in graduated sets. There were inkstands, candlesticks and card racks, ample footbaths with large matching jugs, colourful chamber pots and dainty 'sprinkling bottles' for lavender water. Then there was a range of tall decorative vases in the Chinese style with dragon handles. Mason's even extended its Ironstone ware to complete chimneypieces, ambitiously moulded and finely painted.

Marks on Mason's Ironstone can give a reasonably accurate idea of date. Pieces made between 1813 and 1815 bear the mark 'Patent Ironstone China' impressed within a circle. Between 1815 and 1825, the mark 'Mason's Patent Ironstone China', impressed into the clay in one, or two, lines, was

used. From a little before 1820, a printed mark was introduced. It consisted of a crown with 'Mason's' above and 'Patent Ironstone China' below; with variations to the crown, this mark was used until the 1960s. 'Mason's Patent Ironstone' is the mark currently in use.

The most valuable pieces of Mason's Ironstone are, of course, the fine examples dating from the earlier years of the factory's production. Of these, the dinner and dessert services and the best of the tall Chinese-style vases are the most expensive.

Smaller sets and single pieces from Mason's more modest ranges are still quite widely available. Complete sets of octagonal jugs are now rare and highly prized, although single jugs can still be found and are very collectable. Short sets of plates and other single pieces of tableware, even from Mason's later periods, are also worth buying. More recent single pieces, dating from the end of the 19th century, can be bought very cheaply. Across the range, pieces decorated in a single transfer-printed colour will be cheaper than those with gilding and classic Mason's oriental-style decoration.

▲ *A pair of Ironstone plates dating from c.1820, both showing painted rural scenes of the British countryside. Similar views were often used on porcelain dessert services.*

◀ *Unusually-shaped vase with a delicately-painted oriental design and a gilded, six-sided rim, dating from c.1815. An impressive range of vases were produced by the Mason's Manufactory, some of which came in sets of three.*

---

·PRICE GUIDE· **MASON'S IRONSTONE CHINA**

*Single polychrome pieces of tableware are priced at about £50, and larger pieces, such as meat dishes, £150-£200. Complete or part dinner services start at £800-£1,000 and reach £9,000. Large decorative vases are worth £300-£400. Most pieces in pairs are worth more than their single value. Sets of jugs command prices in the* £800-£1,000 *bracket, with pairs fetching £200-£400 and singles £50-£75. Cracked, crazed or repaired Mason's Ironstone is still valuable, particularly early 19th-century pieces, although damage will affect price. Across the range, earlier well-painted pieces are generally valued more highly than later ones.*

# The Victorian Town Kitchen

Warm, cosy and full of delicious cooking smells, the
Victorian town kitchen was an exclusive domain run by
the cook

The spacious kitchen of the Victorian town house was a hive of activity from dawn to dusk. The Victorians had few of the labour-saving devices available now – the lengthy preparations were completed by hand – so a well-organized kitchen was essential.

Kitchen designers of today would find the layout of the Victorian kitchen hard to fault. All the activity was centred around the huge cooking range and the central kitchen table. Pots, pans and utensils were stored on easily accessible low shelves, or hung within reach, while all the food was kept in a large cool pantry. This organization meant that several staff could work in different parts of the kitchen at the same time, washing vegetables, peeling fruit, roasting meat or preparing desserts without getting in each other's way.

For those with sufficient space, the Victorian kitchen is an ideal model to follow when planning and laying out a modern kitchen. Today's solid fuel stoves, for instance, provide a good and more authentic alternative to gas and electric cookers.

*Even in a modern house, a Victorian-style kitchen can look extremely effective and provide a showcase for period collections.*

Bridgeman Art Library

*◀ The well-equipped kitchen of the large Victorian house was busy from dawn to dusk with extensive preparations for breakfast, lunch and dinner. Any spare time was spent making extra cakes and pastries, which were always appreciated, especially for afternoon tea.*

*▼ Simple wooden chairs were kept tucked beneath the large kitchen table for the staff to use at mealtimes.*

In the large terraced houses of the 1850s and 60s the kitchen was situated in the basement at the front of the house, for easy access to the street. The plan of the house allowed for a number of smaller rooms around the kitchen. It usually had a separate scullery with its own shallow stone sink, draining board and wooden draining racks. A walk-in pantry away from the heat of the kitchen range was a necessity, as fresh food quickly went off in the warm atmosphere of the kitchen.

In the absence of a wine cellar – the preserve of the very grand houses – wine was stored beneath the front steps. Opposite, in the tiny front yard, was the shute leading to the coal hole, where the mountain of coal necessary for heating the kitchen range and other fires throughout the house was stored.

The kitchen floor was stone flagged, boarded or tiled, and always kept scrupulously clean. So, too, were the white limewashed walls – hygiene was considered by most cooks to be of prime importance.

### THE KITCHEN RANGE

The big cast-iron range in the fireplace was the central feature of the Victorian kitchen, and, at the time, was a modern invention. These ranges were sometimes known as Rumford ranges, after Count Rumford who had devoted a great deal of scientific ingenuity to the development of flues for coal-burning

kitchen ranges at the end of the 18th century.

These great cast-iron machines were the bane of the kitchen maid's life. The fire, which burned all day long, was left to go out at night, and every morning she had the task of cleaning it, sifting the ashes, then re-laying and lighting the fire before any other duties could be undertaken. The cast iron had to be cleaned with black lead, which was rubbed in, then brushed and buffed with a felt pad. The brass

*▶ An antique butcher's table provides the central feature in this modern kitchen, which is laid out in the Victorian style.*

*◀ Even the most functional kitchen utensils were beautifully designed, such as this attractive brass colander.*

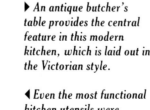

fender around the range also had to be polished, and the maid would often rise before dawn in order to complete these tasks.

### COOKING AT THE RANGE

It was not until late in the 1870s that the closed range, with a flat hot plate over the fire and a better controlled oven beside it, took over from the open version. Until then, the oven temperature had been unpredictable, and baking had to be done in a separate bread oven.

Such advances in cooking facilities made life easier for the kitchen staff, although improvements in the standard of cooking depended very much on the skills of the cook and the budget with which she had to buy the food. Many families expected their staff to perform miracles with the cheapest vegetables and poorest cuts of meat.

Meat was cooked by roasting it on the open fire at the centre of the range, and this necessitated a whole range of equipment, including two vitally important items – the bottle jack and the hastener. The bottle jack was a clockwork device that enabled the joint to be hung vertically before the fire and rotated to ensure even cooking. The hastener – a sort of hooded screen – stood in front of the meat during the roasting, reflecting the heat and catching the dripping in a container at its base, as well as protecting the cook from the heat. Once the meat was cooked it

could be kept warm in the hastener before it was carried upstairs and served to the family in the dining room.

A heavy cast-iron stockpot was always kept simmering on the range to ensure a constant supply of soups and broths. Each night the stock was emptied into a crockery container, and each day it was returned to the pan to heat up again. Even though much time was spent on its presentation, food was generally simple, featuring boiled vegetables,

▲ *Wealthy families sometimes employed as many as ten kitchen staff, who were all busily occupied with the lengthy preparations necessary for large meals.*

---

### LIFE AND LEISURE

## *Kitchen Gadgets*

THE MID-19TH CENTURY SAW THE IN-TRODUCTION OF A WIDE RANGE OF KITCHEN GADGETS DESIGNED TO MAKE LIFE EASIER FOR THE COOK AND HER KITCHEN STAFF. ADVERTISEMENTS ABOUNDED FOR THESE NEW AND IN-GENIOUS INVENTIONS, AND SOON NO VICTORIAN KITCHEN WAS COMPLETE WITHOUT AN ARRAY OF MINCERS, CHOP-PERS, SLICERS AND CORERS. MANY OF THESE ITEMS ARE STILL MADE TODAY.

▶ *The clamp-on mincer introduced in the 19th century proved to be one of the most successful of all Victorian gadgets.*

Liebig "COMPANY'S" Extract of Be

This Signature on Each
FINEST MEAT FLAVOURING STOCK
FOR SOUPS SAUCES AND MADE DISHES
BEWARE OF IMITATIONS.

▲ *The apple-corer was a blessing to any kitchen maid given the task of preparing fruit for an apple pie, but the apple peeling machine was considered somewhat frivolous, so the peeling was usually done by hand.*

◀ *In addition to the many gadgets available, useful flavourings such as beef stock were conveniently packaged.*

▲ *Gadgets designed to cut citrus fruits were a boon when it came to making preserves and marmalades for the family.*

▲ *In large households, the servants might be fortunate enough to eat in a separate room off the kitchen. As a special treat on Sundays, cook would bake them a cake to have with their afternoon tea.*

▼ *A huge clock set high on the kitchen wall enabled cook to time the various meals she prepared and also to keep a check on the punctuality of the kitchen staff.*

steamed puddings and dishes such as stews which could be cooked slowly in side ovens, in addition to the roasts.

### SIMPLE FURNISHINGS

The kitchen furniture was simple and functional. In the centre of the room stood the large main table with its scrubbed deal or pine surface and simply turned legs. The table was used for preparing food but it was regularly cleared for the staff to have their meals. Larger tables were often made with a shelf between the legs known as a pot board, where large cooking pots and pans were stored.

Above the table hung a large rectangular frame where kitchen utensils were hooked ready for use. Despite the apparent simplicity of the kitchen, everything was carefully arranged to make the best use of the space provided – efficiency was essential when there were several people working in the room at the same time.

The kitchen crockery was arranged on a large pine dresser which stood along one wall. The base of the dresser contained spacious drawers for cutlery and cloths, below which was a storage space for big stoneware jars and less frequently used pans.

It was not an infrequent occurrence for junior kitchen staff to sleep in this space beneath the dresser when there was no room in the servants' quarter. This was not as barbaric as it sounds, as at least the kitchen was warm, which is more than could be said of the upstairs bedrooms.

In bigger kitchens one or more side tables would stand against the walls, along with the variety of hard-seated chairs needed to seat the staff of the household at meal-times.

Meals were fitted in between those of the family and, on occasions when the family was entertaining, could be quite sumptuous, although strict economy did not generally allow for too many leftovers.

### COOK'S DOMAIN

In her white starched cap and apron, cook ruled the kitchen with a rod of iron. Her first task of the day was to visit the mistress upstairs and discuss the meals to be prepared, along with any special details such as dinner party menus.

The kitchen was cook's domain, and rarely did the master or mistress cross the threshold, let alone express a preference as to which tradesmen to patronize. Cook preferred to do her own shopping, selecting the best food that her budget allowed.

The staff of the household ate their meals at the scrubbed kitchen table, presided over by cook. Allowances were strictly laid down – bread and butter for breakfast, with bloaters or bacon on Sundays, meat and vegetables or cold meat and pudding for dinner, bread and butter for tea (with jam as a treat) and bread and cheese for supper. Milk, tea, sugar and beer were also provided.

Days were long, although not always unpleasant for kitchen staff, who had the warmth of the range in long cold winters, and food which, although simple, was always adequate. A good employer could keep staff for many years, despite the low wages paid, as good conditions and kindly treatment were always appreciated.

# Stocking the Larder

THE CORNER SHOP SUPPLIED MANY OF THE GOODS NEEDED IN THE VICTORIAN KITCHEN. FLOUR, SAGO, RICE, SPLIT PEAS AND SO ON WERE ALL SOLD FROM BIG SACKS AND TAKEN AWAY IN PAPER BAGS OR CORNETS. SUGAR WAS SOLD IN LUMPS, AND THE GIANT 14LB LOAVES WERE EITHER CUT OR SOLD WHOLE, TO HANG IN NETS FROM THE KITCHEN CEILINGS.

ICE SELLERS DELIVERED TO THE HOUSE DAILY, AND THE ICE WAS KEPT IN ZINC-LINED WOODEN BOXES INSULATED WITH A LAYER OF CORK OR CHARCOAL.

FRESH FRUITS AND VEGETABLES — THE PRODUCT OF MARKET GARDENS — WERE BOUGHT FROM HAWKERS AND BARROW BOYS, OR AT THE LOCAL MARKET.

▲ *Meat and poultry were available from covered markets, to which cook made regular forays.*

▲ *Discriminating cooks were the bane of the stallholder's life, meticulously examining the food and haggling over prices.*

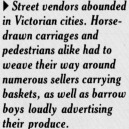
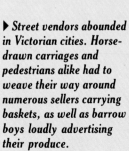

▲ *A barrow boy's success depended on his cry — the louder he called the more people he attracted to buy his goods.*

▶ *Street vendors abounded in Victorian cities. Horse-drawn carriages and pedestrians alike had to weave their way around numerous sellers carrying baskets, as well as barrow boys loudly advertising their produce.*

# Victorian Tiles

Brilliantly coloured and patterned tiles
were among the most beautiful of
Victorian artefacts to adorn walls, floors
and furniture

The Victorians revived the art of tile-making which had almost died out by the early 19th century. In fact, tiles became so popular that their use was extended from floors to walls, fireplaces and washstands. Their glazed surfaces were easily cleaned, so tiles were often incorporated into the design of kitchens and bathrooms. Shops too, especially grocers, butchers and dairies, tiled their walls with spectacular moulded tiles and transfer-printed friezes.

Victorian tiles were available in an almost infinite variety of patterns and, because they were securely fixed to walls, floors and furniture, many have survived. This is good news for the collector: there is a great deal of choice and prices are often low.

### MAJOR MANUFACTURERS

The greatest Victorian tile manufacturer was Minton of Stoke-on-Trent. They published their first catalogue in 1842. This was little more than a pamphlet and only 96 designs were illustrated. By the 1870s, however, Minton's beautiful coloured catalogues showed many hundreds of tile designs from which builders and home owners could choose.

Other Victorian makers to look out for include: the Campbell Tile Company, also of Stoke-on-Trent; Craven Dunhill; Godwin, who tiled the 13th century chapterhouse of Salisbury Cathedral; Doulton; and Wedgwood. Another large manufacturer was Maw and Company of Broseley, Shropshire, who later moved to Jackfield, near Ironbridge. By the turn of the century Maw had overtaken Minton as the largest producer of tiles in Britain.

### A WEALTH OF PATTERNS

The 1840s and 1850s were the decades of the Gothic Revival. Consequently, many Victorian tile designs were based on medieval originals. Pugin, the co-designer of the Houses of Parliament and the foremost proponent of the Gothic style, designed some of Minton's earliest tiles. Besides medieval-inspired designs, Victorian tiles were sometimes based upon Persian originals. Classical and Shakesperian scenes, sometimes produced as a panel with four tiles making up the complete design, were also common.

Later in the century, in the 1880s, the fashion for things Japanese was reflected in tile design. Influenced by the ideals of the Arts and Crafts movement, William De Morgan also produced richly coloured tiles, inspired by Persian motifs and

▲ *The wealth of colour and detail found in Victorian tiles is spectacular. Floral designs were the most popular, followed closely by geometric patterns, all in a variety of rich colours.*

patterns, which were both made and beautifully decorated by hand.

Flowing designs depicting plants, birds and stylized flowers in the Art-Nouveau style were mass-produced at the turn of the century and these became part of the everyday suburban interior. In fact, the scope of tile patterns was so broad that it is no surprise at all to find a 19th century tile – such as one

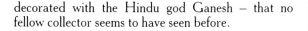

▲ *Many manufacturers are now producing reproduction Victorian tiles which can be used to great effect in period-style bathrooms today.*

▼ *Tile panels were especially popular, and many featured nursery and fairytale scenes, such as this panel by William Morris depicting Beauty and the Beast.*

The encaustic process involved inlaying different colours of clay – with the aid of dies or moulds – onto the surface of the tile, which was then fired. This method was developed during the Middle Ages, but it was 'rediscovered' by Samuel Wright from Skelton, near Stafford, who sensibly took out a patent in 1830. Later, Minton became the major manufacturer of encaustic tiles. As they were very sturdy, these tiles were used for floors and sometimes even for paths outdoors. Frequently, encaustic tiles were glazed, although this made them rather unsafe if they were used as floor tiles as the surface was extremely slippery.

Because of the nature of the process, encaustic tiles were usually fairly simple in design. They are

decorated with the Hindu god Ganesh – that no fellow collector seems to have seen before.

## TYPES OF TILE
The vast range of decorative patterns found in Victorian tiles were almost always produced by one of three methods: the encaustic process, transfer-printing or moulding.

▲ *This striking tile panel was designed by William De Morgan and can be seen in Leighton House, London. The hand-painted tiles together form a picture of birds and flowers in brilliant tones of blue, green and yellow. De Morgan took much of his inspiration from Persian designs. Panels such as these are rare, and highly sought-after by collectors.*

▶ *It is generally fairly easy to identify the method by which tiles were produced. The top tile is an encaustic tile – the geometric pattern is formed using three simple colours. The tile in the centre has a raised moulded pattern in the form of marigolds with stylized leaves, and the third tile, bottom, is transfer-printed with a blue floral design.*

most easily recognized by their colour, usually buff on a terracotta ground, but black, green, blue and white were also used. Collectors particularly admire encaustic tiles incorporating a multiplicity of colours – you can find up to nine forming a pattern on a single tile.

Nearly all the major manufacturers made transfer-printed tiles. Sometimes these were produced in such a way as to resemble the more expensive encaustic tiles. But usually manufacturers exploited the more flexible transfer process to the full and produced tiles in a very wide range of colours and styles. In terms of design, Victorian transfer-printed tiles can be of the very highest quality.

Moulded tiles are usually of a single colour, that is, the colour of the glaze. The colours are often rather sombre, such as rich maroons and dark greens. But Minton made moulded tiles of a delicate blue that was almost as beautiful as an early Persian tile. The quality of design in moulded tiles was very variable and often they were coarse and crudely naturalistic. Maw, however, produced some very good moulded tiles in the late 1880s which were used in both domestic and commercial situations.

### IDENTIFICATION AND DATING

Manufacturers generally stamped or printed their names – boldly and proudly – on the backs of their tiles. While identifying the manufacturer of a tile is generally a simple matter, dating it is seldom very

**▲ Here Victorian tiles are used in a fire grate to complement the older blue and white surround and an impressive carved fireplace.**

**◀ Another of William De Morgan's designs, this tile echoes the colours of the panel opposite.**

## COLLECTING TILES

Tiles are a pleasure to collect. They are easy to display and never fade or need conserving like paintings – a wipe-over with the proverbial damp cloth is all that a tile needs to keep it looking bright. You could try collecting tiles on a particular theme. Flowers, birds, animals and landscapes were all represented on tiles. Like stamps, tiles can be collected in large numbers. But whereas a stamp collection can often only be enjoyed by its owner or another stamp collector, a tile collection can be admired and enjoyed by everyone. Moreover, hunting for tiles and trying to unravel the mysteries of this once popular art form are tremendous fun.

easy. Some tile patterns were in production from the 1840s until the end of the century. The large manufacturers published catalogues and these can be seen in some of the major libraries, such as the National Art Library at the Victoria and Albert Museum.

A Victorian tile catalogue is a treasure. They can sometimes be found in antiquarian bookshops, but most booksellers are aware of their value and may well ask as much for a catalogue in good condition as you might expect to pay for a whole collection of tiles.

---

### ·PRICE GUIDE· VICTORIAN TILES

*Tiles are not expensive to collect. It is still possible to assemble an excellent collection without spending more than £5 on each tile. You can sometimes literally 'pick-up' tiles for nothing – if you are lucky enough to come across a Victorian building which is being demolished. A transfer-printed Minton tile will cost £20 to £40, but rare tiles are not necessarily expensive,*

*unless they are by William Morris or his friend, William De Morgan. A good William De Morgan tile will cost about £100 and a complete panel of Morris or De Morgan tiles can command as high a price as a fine painting. Tiles which can be positively ascribed to well known designers, such as William Burges, tend to be more expensive than tiles by anonymous designers.*

# The Kitchen Table

Hidden away for centuries, amid the servants and the
smoke, the kitchen table finally emerged from its neglect
during the Victorian era

▲ *In the days before purpose-built, fitted work
surfaces, the kitchen table was the scene of most
food preparation. Tables were made cheaply
from either local woods or Scandinavian pine, in
sizes to meet the requirements of their situation.*

Go back in time a century or so and
make your way down the area steps
of a Victorian town house. In the
centre of that basement room is the common
denominator of all British kitchens – the
humble kitchen table. With its substantial,
turned legs, and sturdy rectangular pine
top, pale and scoured, it is as instantly
recognizable today as it was then.

## TAKEN FOR GRANTED

An indispensable but unsung workhorse,
the kitchen table is about the least glamorous
article of furniture in the house. Indeed, it is
unusual to find mention of any kitchen
furniture in contemporary accounts of everyday life before the 19th century.

A few writers confirm our suspicions that
where there was food to prepare, there had
to be a surface at which to work. 'In a
kitchen there should be a small table at
which cabbage may be minced,' writes a
12th century domestic scientist. And a 16th
century author adds a thought on bread
making: 'Here also are troughs to keep
meale in and troughs to lay leaven in and
there is a fair table to mould upon.' These
rare glimpses into ancient kitchens are
confirmed by contemporary paintings: a
12th century monk beats a slab of steak at
the square four-legged table; an Elizabethan
kitchen maid plucks a fowl, sitting at a long
side table.

In the crowded halls or tiny cottages of
medieval England, where living space
served many functions, a table, though
necessary, was something of a space-
consuming luxury. Kitchen tables therefore,
like dining tables, were often made to be
quickly dismantled.

During the 16th and 17th centuries, the trestle table gradually gave way to a design that has survived to the present day: four separate legs joined to a frame, upon which rests the top. There may be reinforcing stretchers between the legs; there may be any amount of decorative carving, but the idea was a successful one and was the basis of a number of familiar designs, from Elizabethan refectory tables to today's self-assemble coffee tables.

The increasingly prosperous 18th and early 19th centuries led furniture designers to develop new styles and sizes of table for the front rooms of middle-class houses. The unfashionable kitchen table, however, needed only to be strong and serviceable – little more than a rectangular work surface on four legs.

### MATERIAL AND STYLES

Although the shape of the kitchen table changed little in the century prior to Victoria's reign, the material of which it was made underwent a revolution. During the early 18th century, because native timber was in relatively short supply, the vast softwood forests of Scandinavia became the principal source of wood for cheap furniture, as well as for much fine carved work.

In country areas, workmen continued to make kitchen tables from whatever wood came to hand – beech, elm or sycamore perhaps – but by Victorian times pine, or deal as it was called, was used for virtually all 'backstairs' furniture. Such variation as there was in the design of the table depended mainly upon its intended use.

The preparation of food – the chopping, slicing and pounding – was a much heavier and more continual task in a great house than in a small one. Large rectangular tables often had square legs reinforced with stretchers a few inches above floor level. Pot boards, resting on the stretchers, might provide storage space for large kitchen equipment; smaller utensils could be kept in deep drawers built into the frame.

The combination of stretchers and drawers made sitting down to eat at such tables highly inconvenient. In these houses, servants generally ate in their own hall at a simple dining table.

In most middle-class houses, on the other hand, the kitchen doubled as a dining room for the servants. Here, as in small houses with no servants, the table served a dual purpose. It had to be sturdy enough for work but comfortable enough for meals. This generally meant the elimination of stretchers, while shallow drawers ensured adequate knee-room. Where a conventional table was too small for all the backstairs household, a drop wing, supported by a gateleg or hinged brackets, provided extra seating space.

These simple styles of pine kitchen table,

the product of both practicality and neglect, continued with only minor variations throughout the Victorian era.

### VICTORIAN TASTE

Mrs Beeton, who held forth on all aspects of domestic life through many editions of *Household Management,* wrote one stern and comprehensive paragraph on the kitchen table. It 'should be massive, firm and strongly made. It may be furnished with drawers or not . . . The upper surface of the table board should show the natural wood, and, if made of deal, should be kept well scrubbed; the edge of the table board, the frame and the legs should be stained and varnished.' She strongly advised against drop wings, which she considered to be unstable.

Mrs Beeton was writing for the now vast middle-class, who might be able to afford two or perhaps three servants. Their kitchens were small and the tables would almost certainly be for eating at as well as for work. They would be made of North American softwood and mass-produced in furniture factories. Fundamentally, however, they were little different from all the unsung kitchen tables that precede them in history.

▲ *Victorian kitchen tables are sought-after today for use in up-to-date interiors.*

▼ *This museum kitchen (at the birthplace of composer Gustav Holst) shows the typical arrangement of a late Victorian kitchen.*

◄ **DESIGN IN FOCUS** ►

# The Pine Kitchen Table

THE VICTORIAN KITCHEN TABLE IS GENE-
RALLY MADE OF SCANDINAVIAN OR NORTH
AMERICAN SOFTWOOD, TODAY SIMPLY
KNOWN AS PINE. ANY NUMBER FROM
THREE TO SIX PARALLEL PLANKS ARE USED
TO MAKE UP THE TOP, WHICH IS NEITHER
PAINTED NOR STAINED.

LEGS ARE TURNED TO AN UNCOMPLICATED
DESIGN; SQUARE LEGS ARE LESS COMMON.
THEY ARE ATTACHED TO THE FRAME WITH
MORTISE AND TENON JOINTS, SECURED
WITH DOWELS. STRETCHERS BETWEEN
LEGS ARE UNCOMMON ON SMALLER
TABLES.

THERE IS USUALLY A DRAWER AT ONE OR
BOTH ENDS. A SIDE DRAWER SUGGESTS
THAT THE TABLE WAS FOR USE AGAINST
THE WALL. ROUND WOODEN OR WHITE
CERAMIC KNOBS ARE CHARACTERISTIC.

① BARE PLANKS ON THE TABLE TOP.

② GAPS BETWEEN THE PLANKS FROM
SHRINKAGE OF THE SURFACE WOOD.

③ WOODEN KNOB ON DRAWER.

④ TURNED LEGS, TRADITIONALLY
STAINED OR PAINTED.

⑤ THE JOINT BETWEEN LEG AND FRAME
IS SECURED WITH A DOWEL.

## Local Woods

BEFORE IMPORTED PINE BECAME A MAINSTAY FOR 'BACKSTAIRS'
FURNITURE, COUNTRY JOINERS USED LOCAL WOODS, SUCH AS
FRUITWOODS, BIRCH AND ELM (BELOW).

The pine kitchen table is the Cinderella of the antique market, having graduated from the drudgery of the Victorian kitchen to become the admired centrepiece of today's dinner party.

Not just any kitchen table qualifies for today's high regard – and high prices. The piece now especially prized once belonged to an unpretentious middle-class family whose two or three servants practically lived at the table – preparing food, eating meals, and, when work was over, playing cards.

Because the pine table's simple design has been so long-lived, exact dating is not always easy. Nor, in terms of price, is it particularly important – a robust Victorian model is of greater value than a rickety Georgian one.

There are, however, certain general indications of a table's age. Early versions are more likely to have straight legs and may be recognized by wider planks on the surface. A top with three 10in (25cm) planks is likely to be Georgian; one with five 6in (15cm) planks is probably Victorian.

The joinery also gives a rough clue to a table's age. Drawers of late Victorian tables often fit

# ·PRICE GUIDE· ⟩ *Kitchen Tables*

UNUSUAL EARLY VICTORIAN PINE TABLE WITH TWO CONVENIENT DOUBLE-ENDED DRAWERS.

PRICE GUIDE ❼

ATTRACTIVE VICTORIAN PINE TABLE WITH SLENDER, CHAMFERRED LEGS AND DOUBLE DRAWERS.

PRICE GUIDE ❺

SIMPLY ORNAMENTED SYCAMORE TABLE, WITH SQUARE LEGS AND SHORT STRETCHERS, C. 1850.

PRICE GUIDE ❽

STANDARD PINE TABLE WITH TWO DROP-LEAVES AND SHORT STRETCHERS. POSSIBLY A 'MARRIED' PIECE.

PRICE GUIDE ❸

SYCAMORE KITCHEN TABLE WITH BRASS-HANDLED FRONT DRAWER AND TAPERING, SQUARE LEGS.

PRICE GUIDE ❻

VICTORIAN PINE TABLE WITH TYPICAL SIDE DRAWER AND DOVETAIL JOINTS BETWEEN PLANKS.

PRICE GUIDE ❻

together with small and regular machine-cut dovetails. Georgian and early Victorian drawers are made with rougher hand-cut dovetails or simple, nailed butt joints.

Look also at how the legs are attached to the frame. Generally, a tenon in the frame slots into a mortise in the leg; this joint is secured with dowels or hand-made pegs driven through the leg into the tenon. If you see no sign of dowels, the table is probably of relatively late manufacture.

When buying a kitchen table, check that its drawers run smoothly, that it stands firmly on the floor and that its leg joints show no sign of separation from the frame. Make especially sure that it is high enough: Victorians were shorter than we are. For comfortable seating, look for a clearance of 24in (60cm). The feet of Victorian kitchen tables have often rotted after years on damp floors and dealers frequently splice an extra inch or so to the legs of an over-low table to give added height.

Although its price has increased dramatically in the last ten years, a genuine Victorian table still costs less to buy today than a good reproduction. Various sizes are available, with or without drawers or drop wings, but an antique round table is expensive and hard to find. Sadly, it is no longer possible to follow the advice of a Victorian guide to household management which cheerfully suggested that a round table could be made to order for 'no more than a pound'.

## REAL OR FAKE?

■ Wide table-top planks suggest early date.

■ 'Frayed' feet, dented or marked legs point to antiques rather than reproductions.

■ A plywood drawer base is a recent replacement.

■ Machine-made dovetail joints in drawers are typical of late Victorian work.

■ No sign of dowels or pegs joining leg to frame suggests recent work.

■ Old tables often develop gaps between the boards on top.

# The Preserving Pan

One of the most important tasks of the Victorian cook was to preserve summer produce for the cold winter months. For this a gleaming preserving pan of silver, copper or brass was essential

Vegetables and fruit were plentiful in Victorian towns. Many areas now close to town centres were then open land with productive market gardens, each with its own speciality – raspberries, currants, strawberries and so on – to which people made pleasant outings in the summer months. In London and other cities a wide range of home-grown fruit and vegetables, as well as some imported produce, were available, while small towns had the benefit of fresh, locally grown produce, if not the same variety.

The only problem was that produce was more or less confined to its own season. Today, refrigeration and air transport have made the effect of the seasons almost negligible but in the 19th century, one of the cook's tasks was to preserve gluts of low-priced summer produce and store them for winter.

### SILVER, COPPER AND BRASS PANS

To enable the Victorian cook to capture the delicious tastes of summer in jams, jellies and chutneys, a large preserving pan was essential. The design of this has changed little, if at all, over the years. A wide pan, with straight or outward-sloping sides allows the excess water in the fruit to evaporate quickly. A metal of good conductivity ensures that the jam cooks evenly and reaches its setting point quickly.

Some households had treasured preserving pans which were handed down from mother to daughter for generations. New ones, however, were the lot of most people and these still make covetable antiques today. Lucky housewives had silver pans, and these are said to have been a wonder to use, as the conductive properties of silver are excellent. Silver

also leaves the flavours of food completely untainted.

Copper, a cheaper alternative, is again a good conductor of heat and was the preferred choice for most cooks, even though it dented easily. Copper saucepans were generally lined with tin, as copper can react and be toxic with some foods, but preserving pans were never lined. There were two

---

### THEN AND NOW

## Bitter Orange Marmalade

THIS TRADITIONAL SCOTTISH RECIPE USES SEVILLE ORANGES TO PRODUCE A MARMALADE WITH A STRONG, CLEAR JELLY.

1.5kg/3lbs Seville oranges     (Makes 4.5kg/10lb)
3kg/6lbs sugar
3.4L/6pts water

Score rind of each orange into quarters and peel off. Slice thinly into small chips (approx. 1cm long). Chop pulp into pieces, removing seeds. Set aside a small quantity of water from the total, add seeds and leave to steep. Put rind and pulp into a basin, boil remaining water and pour over. Leave for 12 to 14 hours, then turn into a large pan. Press soaked seeds through a sieve and add to fruit along with their water. Boil the entire mixture until rind is tender, then gradually add sugar. Boil until mixture jellies. Pour into jars and seal.

*◄ Although pots and pans were washed and dried as soon as possible after use, a weekly polishing was advisable to keep tarnishable metals bright. The outsides of pans used over open fires often suffered from a build-up of smoke and soot, but this could be removed with the help of a good proprietary cleaner.*

*◄ An extensive range of preserves could be made with the aid of a large, shallow preserving pan. Delicious fruit jams, clear jellies and syrup compotes were prepared from a whole range of fruits and in sufficient quantity to keep the larder well-stocked throughout the cold winter months.*

*▼ The pickling and preserving of fruits and vegetables was initially carried out for reasons of convenience. The taste for these traditional foods, however, was eventually catered for by a growing number of food manufacturers. Towards the end of the 19th century, bottled and tinned foods became more and more widespread and could be bought at most corner shops.*

reasons for this: first, the large quantity of sugar in jams and jellies rendered the copper completely safe; and secondly, the melting point of tin is only just above the boiling point of sugar.

Brass or alloys of copper and tin, such as bronze or bell metal, were the choice of women on lower budgets. These metals made adequate preserving pans, but they lacked the conductive qualities of silver and copper.

## EARLY PRESERVES

The preserving of food was not new to the Victorians, and has an extremely long history. It began as a complete necessity when, from lack of winter fodder, most livestock was slaughtered during the autumn and the meat then salted or sometimes smoked to make it last. Vegetables were in short supply in winter, so beans and pulses were dried while they were plentiful.

Preserves had also long been enjoyed for their own sake: a quince 'marmelada' filtered through from 12th century Portugal, and the Crusaders brought back sealed stoneware pots of orange and lemon peels preserved in sugar. Spices – useful for flavouring the salted meats – were also popular from the Middle Ages.

The ancient technique of pickling in vinegar became popular in 17th century England when the tax on salt made it impossibly expensive. In the following century the British began bottling fruit and turning it into jams and jellies.

By the 19th century, preserving was not so much a necessity as a prudent pleasure. After all, alternative fruits and vegetables were available all winter and commercially prepared preserves could now be bought at the corner shop. But many town-dwellers had country roots, which were very much in evidence in the rituals of jam-making and pickling.

## PICKING AND BUYING PRODUCE

For pickles and chutneys, imperfect fruits and vegetables may be carefully picked over, and damaged bits removed, but for marmalades, jams and syrups, fruits must be at their peak. Eliza

▲ A FINE QUALITY SHEET COPPER PRESERVING PAN WITH TWO SIDE HANDLES OF SOLID BRASS. BRASS, ITSELF USED FOR PANS, WAS A LESS EFFICIENT HEAT CONDUCTOR THAN COPPER.

▲ A HEAVY SHEET BRASS PRESERVING PAN WITH IRON SWING HANDLE. AFTER 1850, PANS WERE FREQUENTLY MADE OF ENAMEL ON IRON, THOUGH THESE WERE SAID TO BE LESS EFFICIENT.

▲ *With the yearly abundance of home-grown, autumn fruits it was essential to avoid wastage by careful packing and storing, in addition to preserving.*

Acton, writing in 1845, recommended firmly that fruit 'be gathered always in perfectly dry weather, and be free from both the morning and the evening dew'. It was difficult for a town-dweller to ensure this, but the trusted cook had the responsibility of rejecting anything with signs of mould, bruising or broken skin, and choosing only the finest, slightly underripe fruit.

'Shopping', for example, at the draper's, was a ladylike occupation, but 'marketing' was the work of the cook. In smaller towns there would be a twice-weekly open market, but in London the many street markets were open every day, selling the produce of the market gardens. Fruit shops and greengrocers hardly existed before the end of the 19th century, although the local grocer sold fruit when it was plentiful. Some market gardeners had their own stalls, while hawkers with enormous laden baskets would sell their 'cherry ripe' or 'ripe strawberries' in the streets; but mostly the sellers were barrow boys and market stall-holders who bought from Covent Garden and the other big wholesale markets.

### TYPES OF PRESERVE

There were various sorts of preserving that might be done in the home, as summarized by Mrs Beeton in 1861. Apple rings, plums, mushrooms and herbs were dried; pineapple pieces crystallized in sugar syrup; vegetables pickled; meats salted; and fruits steeped in spirits. But most contemporary recipes, including Mrs Beeton's, concentrate on sugar and vinegar preserves. Chutneys, which contained both

sugar and vinegar, as well as spices, were popular in the 19th century.

All sorts of fruits were preserved in syrups and the kitchen or scullery maid was kept busy, peeling, coring and de-stoning. Orange peel was laboriously sliced for marmalade, while jams and jellies were made from plums, damsons, raspberries, gooseberries, quinces, strawberries and currants, all of which had to be hulled or topped and tailed. Currants were pretty when preserved in syrup on their bunches, then dried out in a moderate oven and strewn with yet more sugar.

For pickles there were lemons, little onions, red cabbages, cauliflowers, walnuts, mushrooms and gherkins. And with the pickling vinegar went spices, some of which were grown at home (saffron from

▲ *Tall glass preserving jars gradually succeeded earthenware versions. These had tin screw-lids with glass seals.*

PRICE GUIDE ❶

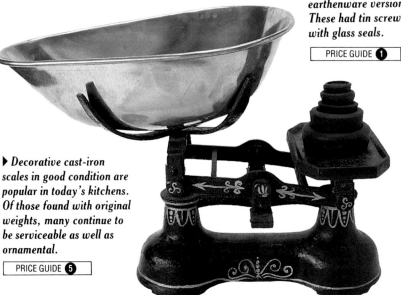

▶ *Decorative cast-iron scales in good condition are popular in today's kitchens. Of those found with original weights, many continue to be serviceable as well as ornamental.*

PRICE GUIDE ❺

50

Saffron Walden in Essex, caraway from Oxford-shire, and mustard from the Fens and the Tewkes-bury area).

Just as the sugar for jams and syrups had to be cut from a big loaf and pulverized by hand, so the nutmegs had to be grated and all the other spices freshly ground by pestle and mortar. So there was much work for the kitchen maids, even before the main operations began.

### PRESERVING EQUIPMENT

The equipment needed for preserving at home was much the same in Victorian times as now. As well as a preserving pan and scales for weighing the ingredients, the cook required brass or iron trivets to rest hot pans on, wooden spoons, a metal ladle and funnel for pouring, and containers for storing. A perforated skimmer with a long handle was used for removing the foam, which was much more copious with loaf sugar.

The handsome kitchen scales with their range of weights and big, wide pan were made of brass or brass and cast-iron. The containers used were often stoneware jars, sealed with thick greaseproof paper and goose grease or mutton fat. However, glass came more and more widely into use during the

period; wide-necked jars and narrower bottles were made of clear or palest blue-green glass, shot through with tiny air bubbles. They were sealed with corks and wax.

There were many recipes for scouring agents to keep all these pans, skimmers, ladles and funnels clean and gleaming. Such recipes included a mixture of silver sand, salt, vinegar and flour, or salt and lemon juice.

Just as it is today, jam making could be completed fairly quickly, once the ingredients had been pre-pared. Marmalades and jellies, however, usually took more than a day. Candied fruits and fruits in syrup took up to four days and involved removing and returning the fruit to the pan several times. Pickling, too, could take several days.

The process of drying and sterilizing the contain-ers in the oven, and keeping them warm if necessary, was enough to harass the best-tempered house-keeper. But when she had corked the last bottle and sealed the last jar, the cook, or the housewife who did her own preserving, must have felt that all her efforts had been worthwhile, as she surveyed the rows of gleaming jars or glazed pots waiting for their labels. Stored in a dark, dry cupboard they would last until the next season – given the chance.

▲ *A long-handled ladle kept the hands clear of scalding steam and was ideal for use with a heavy brass preserving pan.*
PRICE GUIDE ❺❸

▼ *Victorian kitchen scales with round brass tray and solid brass weights. Such examples can be surprisingly costly.*
PRICE GUIDE ❺

▲ *A variety of ceramic preserve jars were used during the 19th century. Shown here from left to right are flat-lidded, salt-glazed, stoneware and drabware versions.*
PRICE GUIDE ❸

▶ *This superb steel pan-stand, complete with a set of graduated copper pans, would have had pride of place in a Victorian kitchen.*
PRICE GUIDE ❽

◀ *Considerable quantities of salt were used in Victorian times for preserving large joints of meat. This attractive salt box with a hinged lid and hole for hanging, is constructed with strips of different coloured woods.*
PRICE GUIDE ❺

# Rolling Pins

Now considered a purely practical piece
of kitchen equipment, the rolling pin
was once a highly decorated
memento that was even given
as a love token

At first sight, the humble rolling pin is one of the most basic items of kitchen equipment, designed first and foremost for the simple task of rolling pastry. Surprisingly, however, rolling pins served a range of other purposes, from the sentimental to the superstitious. Many are highly decorated and inscribed and for this reason, they are among the most interesting and collectable of all kitchen wares.

An inscription could turn a rolling pin into a love token, a souvenir, a charm or talisman, or a memento of a family event. These powers doubtless came from the association of the rolling pin with hearth and home. Although decorated rolling pins could be used, most were too highly prized to be put to the mundane task of pastry-making.

### EARLY ROLLING PINS

Pastry has been made at least since the Middle Ages, and some implement must have been used to roll it flat and thin. Rolling pins as we know them, however, did not come into common usage until the 17th century. From then until the present day, rolling pins have been made in glass, porcelain and wood. Among the earliest were rolling pins of coarse glass; being solid, they were both heavy and cool, and therefore ideal for rolling pastry. Delftware and Staffordshire pottery were other, rarer materials used for rolling pins in the 17th and 18th centuries.

Throughout the 19th century, and probably in earlier times, wooden rolling pins were a humbler alternative to those made in pottery, porcelain or glass. The most commonly used woods were oak, beech, fruitwood, sycamore and walnut, all of which were either stained, lightly polished or left in their natural state.

Most wooden rolling pins had a knob at each end. A refinement was the addition of long or, more usually, short handles; these were either fixed or free-moving, allowing them to rotate as the pin moved up and down the pastry. For impressing a design into shortbread, some wooden rolling pins were supplied with an extra roller, carved with a decorative pattern, which could be interchanged with the more usual, plain roller. Wooden rolling pins with matching wooden potato mashers were sometimes presented as wedding gifts.

### GLASS PINS

Among the most decorative and collectable rolling pins are those made in coloured glass, decorated using various methods. From the end of the 18th century, the Nailsea glassworks near Bristol included among its products glass rolling pins in a range of colours and patterns.

The earliest were dark blue, but the range of colours which soon became available included bottle green, black and opaque white. Effects such as blue and white marbling, mottling, speckling and stippling were also produced. By Victorian times, ruby, turquoise and amethyst had been added to the range. Glass rolling pins were now also made at glassworks in London, Shropshire, Warwickshire, Yorkshire, Stourbridge and Newcastle as well as at Nailsea.

Unlike most wooden examples, few glass rolling pins were perfectly cylindrical. Most had tapering ends finishing with a knob with a rough surface where the molten glass was snapped off as it cooled. From about 1790 onwards, most glass rolling pins were hollow – perhaps originally an economy measure on the part of the glass maker. Some had an opening at one end that could be sealed with a bung; these could be filled with water to give them weight and keep them cool when in use.

Hollow rolling pins had other uses. The practical maid or housewife would fill hers with sugar or salt

*▲ Although not as decorative as glass or china rolling pins, wooden pins are now extremely collectable. From the earliest wooden logs used in the Middle Ages, they developed into well-crafted pieces of kitchen equipment that are often made for a specific task. The two grooved pins shown here are Scottish oatmeal rollers; the one with square holes is for making ravioli. Such pins often came with removable covers so that pastry could be rolled conventionally.*

Most decorated rolling pins also bore inscriptions; the simplest read 'For My Mother' or 'Forget Me Not'; the most elaborate ran to lines of verse invoking heavenly protection for a sailor on a long journey overseas. Commemorative rolling pins bore the date of a marriage, for example, and an inscription wishing the couple happiness and prosperity. 'Love and be happy' expressed a typical sentiment.

As the traditional love token of sailors, glass rolling pins became some of the most popular seaside souvenirs. The 19th century saw the birth of the holiday souvenir trade. The travel industry blossomed as, taking advantage of the railway boom, urban holiday-makers arrived to take the sea air in coastal towns. Their visit was hardly complete without a memento to take home.

### KISS ME QUICK
Decoration on rolling pins exploited the new fashion for souvenirs. Motifs now included soldiers and sailors, policemen, female figures and animals. Inscriptions were also designed specifically with the holiday-maker in mind; 'A Gift from Pwllheli', 'A Brother's Gift from West Hartlepool' and 'Kiss Me Quick' are typical Victorian seaside sentiments that have persisted to the present day. Porcelain rolling pins dating mainly from the 19th century sometimes carried advertisements and recipes. By Victorian times, the principal methods of decorating rolling pins were enamelling, gilding and transfer printing. Enamelling in one or more opaque colours was simple

▼ *While many people collect rolling pins purely for their decorative value, they can, of course, be put to use. This is particularly true of wooden pins, which are less delicate than glass and can be found more cheaply. The woman here is making a traditional apple pie, although the earliest rolling pins were most likely used to make pastry covers, known as 'coffins', in which meat was cooked during the Middle Ages.*

and hang it up in the hearth to keep the precious contents dry. With her rolling pin suspended in the fireplace, the more superstitious woman could rest assured that evil spirits did not visit her house.

### A LOVE TOKEN
Glass rolling pins served other purposes more distantly related to the kitchen and the hearth. Like their wooden counterparts, they were presented as love tokens – very often by sailors to their wives or girlfriends – and the hollow shaft filled with sweets or sugar. For the canny sailor, the hollow rolling pin, with its deceptively sentimental associations, was also a convenient way of smuggling rum, tea or other contraband. It was not unusual for a glass rolling pin to journey with a sailor to the far corners of the globe; suspended in his cabin, it both acted as a talisman on his voyage and served as a reminder of home.

The decoration on these 'sailors' charms', as they were sometimes known, took many forms. The most common motifs were, naturally, a ship in full sail or the open sea viewed through the arch of a bridge. Flowers, leaves and loving couples were other popular motifs.

▶ *Rolling pins were made in a wide variety of materials and shapes, depending on their intended uses. It is possible to make a fascinating collection, which can be displayed to great effect.*

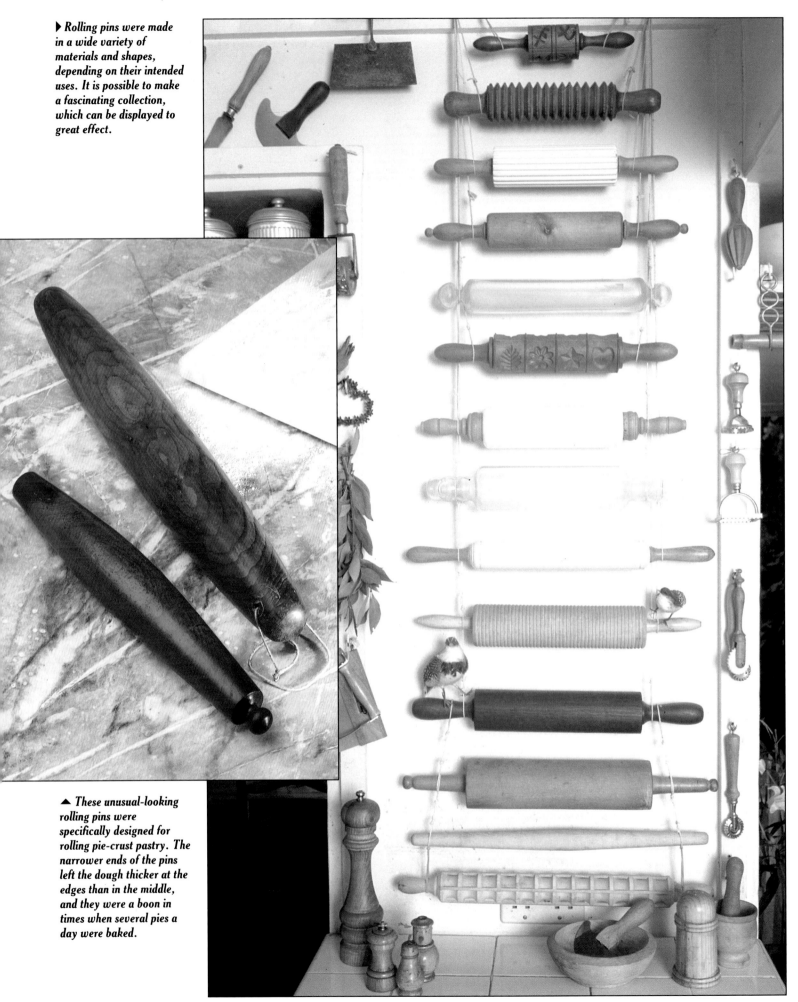

▲ *These unusual-looking rolling pins were specifically designed for rolling pie-crust pastry. The narrower ends of the pins left the dough thicker at the edges than in the middle, and they were a boon in times when several pies a day were baked.*

and effective. It was in fact a more refined and controlled development of mottling and resulted in attractive naive designs with a charming, homespun look to them.

Gilding, by contrast, produced a more refined and sophisticated result. It was most effective on darker colours, where simple designs such as leaves and flowers could be delicately picked out. Enamelling and gilding were, however, both painstaking and time-consuming processes which sooner or later came to be at odds with the increasingly business-like Victorian industry.

### RHYMES AND VERSES

Transfer printing opened the door to speed and mass production. This was by far the quickest, easiest and cheapest method of decorating a china or glass surface. Most Victorian rolling pins are decorated in this way. Relatively complex designs and inscriptions reproduced by the hundreds were simply transferred on to the surface of quantities of rolling pins destined for the popular resorts of Victorian England.

Although it was impractical to use more than one colour for each transfer, single colours could be varied, making the method suitable for every shade of glass. Because of their decorative qualities, glass rolling pins are more collectable than wooden or ceramic ones. Early glass rolling pins predating the era of painted decoration are particularly prized, although they are now quite rare. Deep blue Nailsea pins, dating from between 1790 and 1810 are the most valuable glass rolling pins, followed by those with a marble effect from between 1810 and 1830.

The most colourful and interesting glass rolling pins date from between 1830 and 1860, the height of the Victorian souvenir trade. At the top of the range are those with intricate scenes and verses. Dates referring to a birth or marriage also add interest although flowers and leaves add little to the value. Rolling pins with inscriptions obviously aimed at the Victorian souvenir-buyer are interesting relics of a tradition that lives on today.

Overall, glass rolling pins should have a pure, even colour. Inscriptions and decoration should be clear and delicate. Some rubbing or flaking to gilding or enamel is to be expected, although this should not be excessive. Modern reproductions of decorated glass rolling pins should be easy to spot on account of the freshness of the decoration.

Although they are less colourful and less avidly collected than glass, ceramic rolling pins, particularly those with recipes or slogans, should not be neglected. Homely wooden rolling pins, with no decoration at all, are also worthwhile collectables at the cheaper end of the scale.

▲ *A selection of enamelled, gilded, and transfer-printed rolling pins, two of which are illustrated with advertisements. The deep blue rolling pins were given by sailors as love tokens to their sweethearts and have appropriate messages for both departure and return. On a going-away keepsake, the verse reads: 'Far from home across the sea, To foreign climes I go, While far away O think on me, And I'll remember you'.*

# Cheese Dishes

## The Victorian 'institution' of the cheese course sparked off a variety of attractive designs that are highly collectable today

Eating cheese after dinner became a fashionable habit during the Victorian era, when potteries all over the country were competing to produce the most elegant and functional dishes, both to grace the dining room table and to keep the product fresh. The Victorians bought their cheeses whole, and the full size Stilton dish was a challenge to the best skills of the potter. Today the larger dishes are redundant, since we buy our cheeses in what 'Cook' would consider to be crumb-sized pieces, but they make excellent collectors' items.

Footed salvers and oblong pierced ceramic baskets were made for serving cheese in the 18th century, but they are now extremely rare and most of the dishes to be found on the market date from the 19th and early 20th centuries. The Victorian dishes are of two basic types: the cylindrical Stilton dish with a high, bell-shaped lid and the later wedge-shaped dish which was manufactured in great numbers after about 1870.

### THE INVENTION OF THE CHEESE COURSE

Although cheese was a staple diet during the 18th century, it was the Victorians who instituted the cheese course, eaten after pudding and before the desserts (stewed and crystallized fruits, cakes and other sweetmeats). 'Dinner without cheese is like a woman with one eye,' Mrs Beeton reminded her readers.

To satisfy demand, cheese making intensified and during the mid-19th century England was importing some 100,000 cwt of cheese from America alone. The introduction of cheese factories in 1870 meant that English producers were able to compete with cheap imports by standardizing their own methods of manufacture.

The Victorian cook was spoilt for choice with a whole range of local cheeses whose names are unfamiliar now, including Dunlop, Suffolk, Sage, Brickbat and Double Cottenham. The favourite cheeses though were undoubtedly Leicester, Cheshire, Cheddar and Stilton, made from April to September when the grass was eaten at its best. Cheddar was bought in 'truckles' weighing from 7 to

▶ *By the mid 19th century, the cheese dish commonly held pride of place in the Victorian cupboard or dresser. By 1870, however, the earlier round cylindrical versions had been replaced by rather more practical wedge shapes.*

▲ *This late Victorian cheese dish and cover has been transfer-printed and hand-decorated in blue, then glazed and overpainted by hand in red and gold. Cobalt blue dye was often used as an 'under-glaze' in this way because of its high resistance to heat.*

13lb, though, as an indication of its popularity, Queen Victoria was presented with a Cheddar with a 9ft circumference, weighing in at 11 cwt. Most regal of all, however, was the Stilton cheese, eulogized in the literature of the period, and the most extravagant and fanciful creations of the potteries were reserved for the Stilton dish.

### EARLY DESIGNS

Some of the Stilton dishes and most of the wedge-shaped dishes were made as part of a service and were bought from shops like Thomas Goode and John Mortlock, which were supplied direct by the potteries. The designs reflect changing tastes and fashions throughout the 19th century. A number of early examples were made of bone china, though this material proved a little fragile and the larger dishes were more commonly made of earthenware and stoneware. Before majolica glazes were invented, the dishes were usually transfer-printed.

Very attractive early blue printed ware was made in imitation of the Chinese Nanking pottery. In the 1840s multicoloured transfer printing was introduced, using separate copperplates, and it was common for transfer-printed ware to be overpainted by hand using gold and other colours to highlight the design. Early examples, like the Mason's Ironstone longtail bird service, imitating Chinese *famille rose* porcelain, are now rare collectors' items.

### DECORATIVE MOTIFS

In 1851, Minton's developed the very brightly coloured majolica glazes, so-called because they were loosely thought to resemble Italian Renaissance majolica. The strong blues and greens proved highly popular with the Victorians, and by the 1870s Minton and Wedgwood were employing teams of majolica paintresses decorating cheese dishes with moulded fruit, flowers, leaves and even cows. Motifs referring to the edible accompaniments of the cheese course were also common, such as vine leaf trails and swags of fruit and nuts. On top of the cheese dish lid the knop (or finial) was frequently moulded as a cow.

Cheese dishes from the late 1860s and 1870s reflect the vogue for Japonaiserie. Wedgwood produced services with fanciful names like 'Mikado', 'Satsuma' and 'Imperial Dragon', while Minton manufactured a cheese dish modelled as bamboo sticks and decorated with spiky bamboo leaves. Other motifs included stylized palms and birds perched on springs of oriental blossom. Dudson produced a very smart cheese dish with a shiny black 'Jackfield' glaze, transfer-printed and hand painted, probably in imitation of oriental lacquer.

Wedgwood manufactured Stilton dishes in their highly successful blue and green jasper ware, decorated with classical figures in relief. These are now very rare and expensive, but other factories including Copeland and Dudson made Wedgwood lookalikes in stoneware and undercut the Wedgwood prices. Most of the copies that can be found on the market today were made by Dudson, perhaps the most prolific producers of cheese dishes between 1840 and 1890. The Dudson dishes are distinguish-able by their acorn and cut rope knops and by their range of colours including pale, slate and dark blue, sage green and claret brown. Cherubs, muses and other classical figures were applied in imitation of jasper ware but the Dudson dishes also feature large ferns, birds and butterflies and hunting scenes.

## NOVELTY DESIGNS

Even the most novel inventions of the potteries make good collectors' pieces. William Brownfield at Cobridge specialized in a 'castle' dish – a battle-mented tower decorated with an ivy trail – and Stafford-shire produced a dish in the form of a cow's head with flaring nostrils and a tangled forelock as a handle.

Royal Doulton was one among a handful of potteries which continued to make cheese dishes after World War I. From 1914 to 1928 they introduced their 'series' ware, and the Shakespearean Charac-ters proved very popular. Beswick, a Doulton subsidiary, produced ornamental Cottage Ware throughout the 1920s and 1930s, and it is still possible to find little Mock Tudor 'oake beame' cheese dishes at local antique fairs.

▼ *By the late 19th century cheese dishes had become increasingly functional – in this example, the hitherto popular knop has been replaced with the more conventional handle. The floral pattern reflects the increasing Victorian preoccupation with nature.*

*◀ The early 20th century saw an influx of wedge-shaped cheese dishes in a range of patterns that today offer enormous scope for collectors. Commemorative ware, as typified by the dish from Clacton on the left, was ever-popular, while the pastel backgrounds and brightly coloured hand-painted flowers in relief of Beswick ware (shown in the two dishes right and front) offered a welcome change from the rather more ornate and formal early Victorian versions.*

*▼ A 1930s Art Deco cheese dish by T. Green and Co. from Gresley, Derbyshire. The strikingly painted flowers are an imitation of the popular Clarice Cliff 'Crocus' design.*

## POST-WAR DECLINE

Both cheese dishes and cheese making suffered from the privations of World War II. Large Stilton dishes became obsolete and hundreds of local cheeses were already extinct. By the 1950s, the dire state of the cheesemaking industry caused an American expert to comment, 'While England may well survive the falling away of her colonies, a falling off in her cheese whispers of some deep and staunchless inner wound.'

## BUILDING A COLLECTION

Stilton dishes can be found in specialist pottery and porcelain shops, but they are relatively rare. Sometimes tops and bottoms are complementary but not in fact the original pair, and this ought to be reflected in the price. Small wedge-shaped dishes can be picked up at most antique fairs and even second-hand shops. There are plenty of themes for a collection: buying from one maker, or one type of decoration such as jasper ware or majolica, or even collecting Japonaiserie or hunting depictions are some suggestions for a starting point. If identification is a problem, most of the Stoke potteries are willing to help with any enquiries.

Discoloration is quite common on cheese plates and applied decoration, but the temptation to remedy it with bleach should be resisted. Seek the advice of professional china restorers, who are also best able to deal with complicated breakages affecting decorative mouldings and glazes. Large Stilton dishes do not fit easily into display cabinets, but anyway look their best – as do the wedge cheese dishes – on a particularly fine Victorian sideboard or pine dresser.

## ·PRICE GUIDE· CHEESE DISHES

As a very rough guide, the plainer wedge-shaped dishes can be bought for £15 to £30 (perhaps even less at a cheap fair) while those with more elaborate rococo shapes and hand-painted decoration may fetch up to £60 or £100. The Stilton dishes are usually around £100 to £250, and the price is affected by the maker, design and condition. The best and rarest dishes from the early 19th century like Chamberlain's Worcester might cost anything up to £450, and you should expect to pay anything from £200 to £300 for early Wedgwood and up to £1000 for elaborate majolica pieces.

# Victorian Food Packaging

Food packaging offers the collector not only a colourful display, but also a fascinating insight into the dawning of the advertising age

In the early years of Victoria's reign, branded packaged goods were a rarity; by its end, they were a commonplace. None of the packages developed in the 19th century have any great intrinsic value, apart from a decorative one, but as a record of the ephemeral, everyday life of a recently bygone age, they make a fascinating subject.

### FROM PAPER TO PACKAGING

The Georgian and early Victorian retailer bought food supplies in bulk direct from the farmer or manufacturer. The only packages were paper bags and tissues supplied by the retailer. The 19th century development of mass-production processes made it possible for the manufacturer to sell his goods in cans, bottles, jars, packets and tin boxes. Responsibility for promotion and sales shifted from the

▲ 'Juvenile' tins developed in the 1890s, where prams, sentry boxes and books were really intended as stocking fillers and just contained token biscuits.

▶ The durable bottles, tins and pottery jars that were used to package food in the late Victorian era, survive in the greatest numbers today.

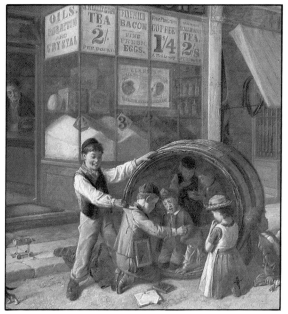

▲ *Victorian grocer's shops sold some pre-packaged foods and also weighed out goods into paper bags.*

shopkeeper to the manufacturer, sowing the seeds of the modern-day advertising industry. For the first time, individual brand names could be established, helped by the Trade Marks Act of 1875.

By the 1880s, manufacturers such as Cadbury's and Crosse and Blackwell had already established several brands. Bovril first appeared in its distinctive bottle in 1886. There were no breakfast cereals except porridge, which was one of the last goods to be branded; Quaker Oats was established in 1899.

Different products required different packaging containers. For example, jam was sold in pots and jars, either earthenware or glass, whereas sweets, custard and mustard were more suited to tins. The most common packaging, however, was the simple cardboard box.

### PROMOTIONAL PACKAGING

At first packaged in functional containers, products were gradually sold in more decorative wrappings. Special gift boxes for chocolates were one of the first to be produced. Cadbury's began the trend – and set the style – in the 1860s with a box featuring a picture of a winsome kitten. So much did the idea appeal to Victorian sentiment that by 1882 Rowntrees alone were producing more than 150 different decorated boxes every Christmas.

Biscuit manufacturers such as Huntley and Palmers were quick to seize on the potential of decorated packs, producing attractive tins for the Christmas market. The first were simple tin boxes with paper glued to the sides.

### DECORATIVE TECHNIQUES

Decorative boxes were produced with enamelled designs; then in 1868 Huntleys produced the first transfer-printed tins. A sheet of transfers was placed face-down onto a prepared tin sheet. The backing was then soaked off the transfers and they were given a coat of copal varnish before being finished with an application of heat. This decorative technique was capable of great subtlety of colour and design and

▲ *Cheaper printing methods meant the simple tin box was soon superseded, and fanciful shapes introduced. Hardy and useful, these chocolate boxes survive in numbers as they have been pressed into service to hold pins, buttons and other knick-knacks.*

with age developed a fragile crackle-glaze finish that enhanced its resemblance to fine porcelain.

Transfer-printing died out after the 1880s as the cheaper and more efficient offset lithographic method was developed. This involved first printing the designs onto flat, glazed cardboard, then offsetting them onto the tin plate. The cheapness of the offset method meant that more and more designs could be introduced.

### DESIGNS AND SHAPES

The standard printed designs were pictures of famous places, children, flowers, birds or prominent people, such as Royalty. Reproductions of Old Masters were used as lids, and came with a hook for hanging up once the contents were consumed.

Special commemorative packets for tea and mustard were produced for events such as the Jubilees of 1887 and 1897. The Union Jack was a popular motif, very often used to combat growing competition from imported branded goods. Famous names and images were often appropriated to sell inappropriate goods, such as Baden Powell whisky and Captain Webb matches.

As the century progressed, biscuit and sweet tins were produced in more exotic shapes. Ovals and ellipses, urns and caskets were popular in the 1880s,

◀ *With the mass-production of hardy food containers, such as tins and bottles, came the age of advertising. Manufacturers promoted their products on the solid packaging and also designed special publicity material.*

while in the 1890s popular lines mimicked baskets of straw or wickerwork, shelves of books, porcelain vases and items of furniture. In fact, the contents had become secondary to the package.

### MAKING A COLLECTION

Victorian packaging is not an easy area for collectors. There are no showrooms and nothing but the best-quality biscuit boxes turn up in antique shops. The excavation of Victorian tips may unearth interesting bottles, jars and pot lids, but paper goods and cardboard, which are the mainstay of packaging, are rare survivors today.

Although there are no particularly collectable items, there are several specialist fields. These include the tins of chocolate sent by the Crown to the soldiers fighting in South Africa as a token of the sovereign's gratitude. They were brought back in great numbers and are a relatively common find.

Dating is a problem as the most popular food brands were sold in packs that varied only slightly, if at all, over the decades. As a rough guide, very early examples have the maker's name as part of the design. By the mid-1880s, this had moved to the base or inside of the lid as the tins had become valued as decorative objects in their own right and advertising on the package was considered vulgar.

---

### ·PRICE GUIDE·     FOOD PACKAGING

*Juvenile and fantasy boxes in very good condition are the most valuable items of food packaging, fetching between £50 and £100, although many fine examples can be hunted down for much less.*

*Embossed bottles are worth a few pence without their labels, and a few pounds with them intact. Everyday tins and boxes for tea, biscuits and*

*chocolates will cost no more than a pound or two, if they can be found at all. The earliest machine-made tins with transfer-printing are generally more valuable than those decorated with offset lithography. The historical interest, fragility and disposability of packets means that condition is not such an important factor in their collectability as it is in other fields.*

# The Victorian Servants' Hall

A warm, spacious room situated in the basement of the
house, the servants' hall was modestly furnished but
provided a place for relaxation

The Victorian *nouveaux riches* modelled their
households on those of the landed aristo-
cracy. Servants, therefore, were more than a
necessity for the smooth running of the house, they
were a status symbol – an important way of
displaying wealth, which the Victorians loved to do.
The more servants you had, the higher your status,
and it was not unknown for families to scrimp and
save on their own comfort and even to go without
food in order to afford a footman or a lady's maid.

The servants' hall was a large but very simply
furnished room and, being near the kitchen, was
always warm. Here the servants ate their meals and
relaxed in whatever time they had between chores.
Here they might enjoy a game of cards or a
conversation, but generally it was not a place of
informality. The rigid hierarchy of Victorian social
life extended below stairs as well as above. Everyone
from the butler down to the youngest maid knew his
or her place, and was expected to keep to it.

*In grand
houses the
servants' hall
was nearly as
large as the
main kitchen;
while the staff
of smaller
households
might not have
had a separate
hall at all.*

◀ Small houses of the middle classes, especially in town, would not have had space for a servants' hall. In this case, the servants would take their meals in the kitchen. The farmhouse, shown here, tended to be more egalitarian because the farmer and his wife worked side by side with their employees in the fields and house. Farmworkers and household servants would dine at a separate table in the dining hall.

There were more domestic servants in Victorian times than ever before. Women especially were entering service in large numbers and, because they commanded lower wages, came to outnumber male servants by about five to one. Consequently, the number of male servants came to be a particularly important measure of status.

The landed gentry required on average some 40 to 50 servants to service their country mansions, but a prosperous pottery manufacturer living in a large town house in Stoke would have made do with between 12 and 15. A writer on domestic economy in 1844 said that an income of between £4500 and £5000 per annum was needed to maintain such an establishment.

▼ A dresser or built-in shelves are ideal for displaying copper pans, jelly moulds and sets of crockery in today's kitchen. Large kitchen tables make excellent work surfaces. Like the kitchen, the servants' hall was a basement room with small barred windows.

▲ A sturdy wooden bench or a settle (a high-backed bench) might take the place of chairs for the lower servants at their dining table. It would be made by a local carpenter.

### BASIC REQUIREMENTS

Cook, parlourmaid and housemaid were regarded as the essential three servants. Then came the kitchen-maid and the nursery maid, if there were children in the house, in which case there might also be a nanny and governess. A coachman and a stable lad looked after the family's transportation. The lady's maid attended on the mistress of the house, and the valet did the same for the master. As a male servant, a footman was much valued, and selected primarily for his good looks and his height. A footman over six feet tall could command several extra shillings in his pay packet, as he would look particularly impressive when accompanying the coach on outings.

Over all the other servants were the housekeeper, usually a formidable lady dressed in black with an immaculate white lace cap and a chatelaine at her waist, and the butler, a still more awesome figure who was always addressed as 'Mr' by the other servants. The housekeeper was called 'Mrs', whatever her marital status.

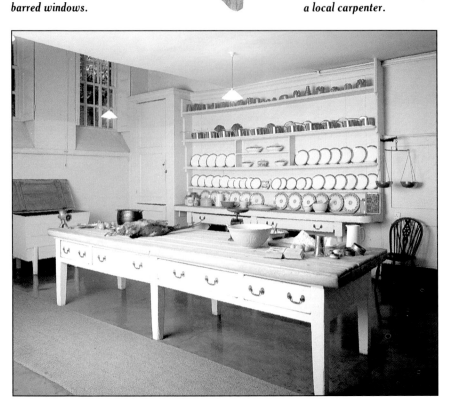

The furniture in the servants' hall was of a basic country variety. There was a long scrubbed pine table and rush-seated, ladder-back dining chairs. The butler and housekeeper had their own rooms in which to relax and perform their duties, and only visited the hall at mealtimes or to give instructions. The next servants in the hierarchy – probably the cook and the valet or footman – would each have had a Windsor chair in the servants' hall, possibly of the low-backed variety known as the smoker's bow, and also perhaps a comfortable armchair.

### MINIMAL DECORATION

Against the wall stood a large dresser for the servants' china. This might also hold one or two decorative items, such as china figures, cottages and sheepdogs that were popular souvenirs of the time, or perhaps a decorated Bristol ware jug and mug. But generally speaking there was minimal decoration in the room.

Gas lighting was being introduced upstairs, but the servants' hall was still lit by candles and oil lamps, probably paraffin or kerosene. There was an open fire in the winter and, because of its proximity to the kitchen range, the servants' hall was usually a lot warmer than the smart rooms upstairs. Central heating was not a feature of the Victorian house.

At all times an eye had to be kept on the wall-mounted service bell board which indicated when someone was ringing for attention, and from which room. Speaking tubes, similar to those used on board ships, made it possible for the family to give orders without actually summoning a servant in person.

### LIFE BELOW STAIRS

The household routine was strict and unvarying and the gruelling round of cleaning and scrubbing the house began as early as 5 a.m. By the time the staff all gathered together for breakfast in the servants' hall around 8 o'clock, a good number of the daily chores were already done. Seated in strict order of precedence, they would consume leftovers from the previous day's roast and cold meat pie, bread and butter, washed down with tea. Although ample, the servants' meal was rather poor in contrast to the huge buffet prepared for the family: eggs, bacon, kidneys, cutlets, chicken and fish, all temptingly presented in chafing-dishes. Work resumed immediately after breakfast for the servants, and all household chores were expected to be finished by midday.

▶ *The speaking tube, which ran from the living rooms to the servants' hall and kitchen, allowed the master and mistress to issue direct orders to their staff.*

---

### ◀ LIFE AND LEISURE ▶

# *Life in the Potteries*

THE SIX TOWNS IN THE AREA OF NORTH STAFFORDSHIRE KNOWN AS THE POTTERIES WERE TUNSTALL, BURSLEM, HANLEY, STOKE-UPON-TRENT, FENTON AND LONGTON. BY 1762 THERE WERE 150 INDIVIDUAL POTTERIES IN THE BURSLEM AREA ALONE, EMPLOYING 7000 PEOPLE.

IN 1769 JOSIAH WEDGWOOD OPENED HIS NEW FACTORY WEST OF HANLEY, CALLING IT ETRURIA AFTER THE CLASSICAL FASHION OF THE DAY. HE USED THE NEW STEAM ENGINES TO DRIVE HIS MILLS, AND WAS INSTRUMENTAL IN BRINGING TURNPIKE ROADS AND THE CANAL TO THE POTTERIES.

IN 1851 THE POPULATION OF THE POTTERIES HAD RISEN TO 100,000. AROUND 750,000 TONS OF COAL A YEAR WERE BEING USED FOR POTTERY PURPOSES, AND £1.7M WORTH OF GOODS WERE PRODUCED IN THE YEAR, OF WHICH £1.3M WENT IN EXPORT, ABOUT A THIRD OF IT GOING TO AMERICA.

◀ WORKERS IN THE PRINTING AND TRANSFERRING ROOM AT ONE OF THE POTTERY FACTORIES. WHERE POSSIBLE, THIS WORK WAS DONE BY MACHINE. ARMIES OF ARTISTS, MAINLY WOMEN, WERE EMPLOYED FOR THE FINER WORK AND FOR FINAL DECORATION.

▲ ETRURIA HALL, WEDGWOOD'S FACTORY IN HANLEY, AROUND 1850. IT IS IN A RURAL SETTING BUT THE AIR IS THICK WITH SMOKE. WEDGWOOD PROVIDED MODEL HOUSING FOR HIS WORKERS. BAD HOUSING AND EPIDEMICS WERE THE NORM ELSEWHERE.

The segregation of servants from family was firmly supported in many Victorian households, and the geography of the house was specifically designed to allow minimum contact. Indeed, in spite of the fact that the Victorians often took pride in their servants from the point of view of status, it was nonetheless rather fashionable to treat them with disdain. Mrs Beeton noted that many employers denigrated their servants at every opportunity: 'It is the custom of "Society" to abuse its servants . . . [and] wax eloquent over the greatest plague in life while taking a quiet cup of tea.'

Generally, the children of the house enjoyed a more relaxed relationship with the servants. While it was almost unknown for the master and mistress to visit the servants' hall, their children might spend odd hours of the day playing there. They could watch the cook at work in the kitchen, help the housemaids to card wool, or listen to the valet's stories of foreign travel and high society.

### LEISURE TIME

By way of their own relaxation (and only with permission from the housekeeper), servants were allowed the occasional afternoon visit from members of their family in the servants' hall. However, these visits tended to be rare, as so many of the servants were recruited from country areas. The hospitality of the servants' hall did not extend to friends, unless a

▲ *A staff of 12 Victorian servants posing for a photograph in 1880. The butler, governess and housekeeper are in the centre. The boys, in their knickerbockers and good leather boots, are probably the children of the house.*

▼ *In their off-duty moments in the servants' hall the staff might pause for a cup of tea with a visiting police constable. Here, one of the maids is raising a laugh with an imitation of the mannerisms of the lady of the house.*

*◄ A cribbage board for scoring at the card game of cribbage which the servants would have played in moments of leisure.*

*▼ The bell board hung on the wall of the servants' hall. This one is manual, operated by the bell pulls upstairs. Later versions were electrical and were activated by push buttons. Shutters opened to indicate which room was calling.*

the more generous masters gave a dance and a feast in the servants' hall, hiring other servants to do the work so that the staff were free to enjoy themselves on that day.

In some households, the servants' hall could be a lively social place at other times too, especially when the butler and housekeeper were safely in their rooms and everyone could relax a bit. At these times the servants would make their own entertainment: perhaps the footman might play the fiddle or penny whistle so that the others could have an impromptu dance, or the valet might know some popular card tricks, picked up on his travels with his master. And in quiet moments, they could always sit and chat as they caught up with their own knitting or sewing.

man had 'serious intentions' towards one of the maids. Even then, he could only pay court to her with the housekeeper's permission.

Work might have been long and hard for Victorian servants, but at least they escaped the appalling filth and poverty that so many others suffered; in service they were assured of a roof over their heads and decent food in their stomachs. And life was not all grind; on Twelfth Night, for instance,

---

◄━ **LIFE AND LEISURE** ━►

## *Mrs Beeton's Life*

ISABELLA MARY BEETON'S *BOOK OF HOUSEHOLD MANAGEMENT* WAS PUBLISHED IN 1861, HAVING APPEARED IN MONTHLY PARTS IN A WOMEN'S MAGAZINE PUBLISHED BY HER HUSBAND. SHE WROTE ON A WIDE VARIETY OF SUBJECTS INCLUDING TRAVEL, PARIS FASHIONS, COOKERY AND OTHER WOMEN'S INTERESTS. HER AIM WAS TO EXPAND MIDDLE-CLASS WOMEN'S HORIZONS AND TO BRING FRESH INTEREST AND DIGNITY TO THEIR DOMESTIC LIFE.

MRS BEETON WAS AN ATTRACTIVE AND PRO-GRESSIVE WOMAN WHO DIED IN CHILDBIRTH AT THE AGE OF 29. THE ELDEST OF 21 CHILDREN, WHOM SHE LARGELY RAISED, SHE HAD FOUR SONS, TWO OF WHOM DIED IN INFANCY.

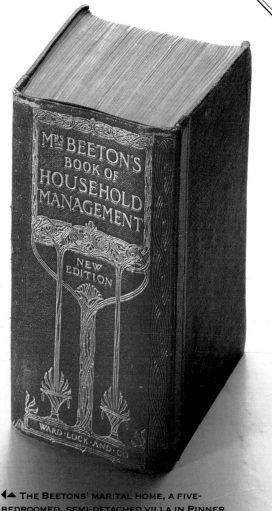

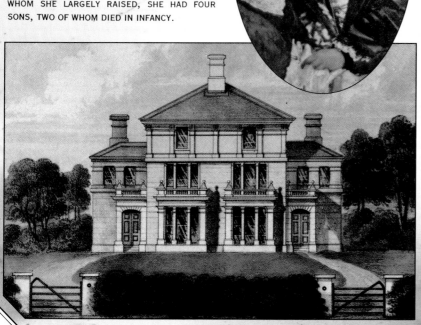

◄▲ THE BEETONS' MARITAL HOME, A FIVE-BEDROOMED, SEMI-DETACHED VILLA IN PINNER. ISABELLA (ABOVE LEFT) BECAME A HOUSEHOLD NAME WITH HER BOOK OF DOMESTIC ADVICE, WHICH IS STILL BEING SOLD TODAY.

# Victorian Farmhouse Kitchen

The centre of farmhouse life, this was the room where the family ate and relaxed and where food was cooked over the fire

When the young Victoria became queen in 1837, the industrial and domestic life of her subjects was in the midst of a period of transition, a time of ever-accelerating change when centuries-old ways of life were overturned in decades. In the kitchen, it was the last pre-gadget era, before canning made much preserving and pickling redundant and before the full power of industrial mass production had been brought to bear on the fashioning of machines to cope with even the most trivial domestic task.

Though almost always at one end of the building, the kitchen was the centre of farmhouse life. It was where the family cooked, ate and, for the most part, lived – the warmest, most cheerful and most heavily furnished room in the house, just as it is in many modern farmhouses. Kitchen furniture and equipment was built to last, and every country kitchen contained sturdy, practical examples of robust country craftsmanship.

For a Shropshire tenant farmer and family in the late 1830s, life was hard but not unsupportable. The small half-timbered farmhouse had its kitchen in a long low room on the east side. Cleanliness was recognized as important, but was difficult to maintain; cooking over an open fire meant that grease, coal-dust and soot got everywhere, and the kitchen had to be regularly sluiced and scrubbed with soap and water. Water was not tapped into the farmhouse, but there was a stand-pump in the yard.

The walls were regularly lime-washed or distempered, perhaps two or three times a year, while the brick floor was scrubbed smooth and worn into soft waves by the passage of time. Just off the kitchen to the north were a cool dim larder where food was kept on stone shelves and a dairy where butter and cheese were made.

## THE HEARTH

Just as the kitchen was the centre of farmhouse life, so the hearth was the heart of the kitchen. It was set against the wall in a deep wide well, tall enough for a man to stand in. The fire itself was contained in an iron basket grate fixed to the back of the hearth by firebars that were cemented into the brickwork. The

◀ *This particularly fine porcelain meat dish, with draining well, held the Sunday roast.*

sides, or cheeks, of the grate were on a rack and pinion so that the width of the fire could be adjusted; attached to the cheeks were iron plates, or hobs, where much of the cooking was done.

The brickwork behind the grate was protected by an ornamental cast-iron fireback that threw heat back into the room. The fire was the only source of heat in the house, and was never allowed to go out. At night it was covered with a low metal dome called a *couvre-feu* or curfew, and the glowing embers were breathed back into life each morning with a bellows or a steel blow-tube.

## KITCHEN FURNITURE

To one side of the fire stood a large basketwork chair, the farmer's own, while on the other was a tall oak settle that acted as high seat, draught excluder and storage space – cupboards under the seat could

▼ *Eggs were stored on racks and kept either in the dairy or the kitchen itself.*

▲ *The farmhouse kitchen had no modern amenities. Water for cooking and washing was brought in from the yard pump.*

be reached from the rear. A rocking chair served the farmer's wife. There was also a large wooden table and benches and a dresser. On the floor, against the walls, were flour barrels and stoneware storage jars.

In the 1830s tea was replacing beer as the national drink, but there was still a brew bubbling quietly next to the brick pillars that supported the stone sink. Bottles of wines and cordials made from field and hedgerow fruits and flowers – cowslips and elder, cherries and sloes – were racked in the larder. Salt was kept in a pine box mounted on the fireplace wall. The beams and rafters were themselves storage spaces. Apple rings, hams, game and nets of dried mushrooms hung near the fire, while cheeses and strings of onions were kept near the cooling draught of the door.

The dishes and plates gleaming on the dresser, mostly inexpensive and attractive ceramics bought from fairs or the nearby market town, also included durable pewter and tin ware and even a few old wooden trenchers. There were pie dishes in tinplate and earthenware, including one or two in Wedgwood's piecrust ware, and jugs, pitchers and serving dishes in stoneware and slipware. Pride of place went to the set of best 'china' from the Potteries.

There was also an earthenware mortar and pestle, used to crush spices, herbs and sugar, copper moulds for jellies, creams and cold puddings, a tinplate mould for shaping cooked puddings and an old set of carved wooden gingerbread moulds.

### COOKING OVER THE FIRE
Food had been cooked over an open fire for centuries. With the advent of chimneys in the 16th century, the fire was moved away from the centre of the room and into a wide hearth against the wall. There would also be a baking oven for cooking the bread and biscuits that formed a large part of their diet. In the poorer households, a small piece of bacon or salt pork with vegetables would be dropped into the pot and maybe dumplings or a rolypoly pudding wrapped in a cloth. However, in the better-off farmhouses, new, flat-bottomed saucepans and kettles of sheet brass, copper or tinplate were to be found. These were rested on the hobs so that a beef or chicken stew could be cooked in one pot and vegetables or broth in another. Although this was relatively simple fare, the separation of sweet and savoury dishes was a new and welcome gastronomic experience for most households.

### ROASTING MEATS
Roasting meat was only a once-a-week affair, except in grand households where a cook and kitchenmaids were employed. On most Sundays a joint of beef or pork was roasted for the family's dinner, which took place at midday. The best plates and tureens which adorned the kitchen dresser were put into service for this substantial meal which usually was taken at the large kitchen table. Home-brewed beer, wine or cider would be served to accompany this hearty meal. Made from hops, apples or berries grown on the farm, this would be the end-product of several weeks' hard work at the end of the summer. The drink would be served on the table in specially decorated mugs and serving jugs. At the beginning of the century spit-roasting was the only method of cooking meat. The old spreading wood fires could provide a wide area of bright heat and accommodate long spits placed horizontally in front of them; one of these spits was kept in the rack above the hearth.

For meat to roast evenly it has to be steadily rotated before a hot fire; once this was done by hand, but it was a hot, hard and tedious job. Above the fireplace and to one side was a recess where once there was a treadmill (small dogs were especially

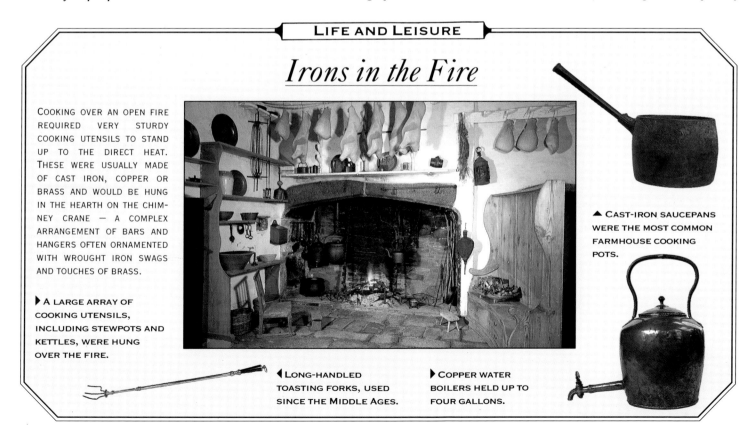

### LIFE AND LEISURE

## *Irons in the Fire*

COOKING OVER AN OPEN FIRE REQUIRED VERY STURDY COOKING UTENSILS TO STAND UP TO THE DIRECT HEAT. THESE WERE USUALLY MADE OF CAST IRON, COPPER OR BRASS AND WOULD BE HUNG IN THE HEARTH ON THE CHIMNEY CRANE — A COMPLEX ARRANGEMENT OF BARS AND HANGERS OFTEN ORNAMENTED WITH WROUGHT IRON SWAGS AND TOUCHES OF BRASS.

▶ A LARGE ARRAY OF COOKING UTENSILS, INCLUDING STEWPOTS AND KETTLES, WERE HUNG OVER THE FIRE.

▲ CAST-IRON SAUCEPANS WERE THE MOST COMMON FARMHOUSE COOKING POTS.

◀ LONG-HANDLED TOASTING FORKS, USED SINCE THE MIDDLE AGES.

▶ COPPER WATER BOILERS HELD UP TO FOUR GALLONS.

new form of spit, with the meat hung vertically from a bottle-jack. Bottle-jacks were patented in 1773; a bottle-shaped cylinder of shiny brass or japanned tin contained a clockwork mechanism that could be wound with a key and would run for over an hour, driving a wheel upon which the meat could be hooked to spin slowly before the fire.

### THE HASTENER

Bottle jacks were used in conjunction with hasteners, or Dutch ovens, half-cylinders which hung from the jack. Their burnished inner surface reflected the fire's heat back on to the meat – and incidentally kept it away from the cook. There was a door in the back of the hastener so that the cook could check on the roast and baste it with a long-handled spoon, using the juices that collected in the copper dripping tray beneath it.

Another essential item of equipment was the dredger, a brass, tin or pewter tankard with a perforated domed lid that was used to shake a pounded mixture of flour, seasoning and spices over the meat to make a coat that helped to hold in its juices and flavour.

It was not only chickens and joints of pig, goat or mutton that were roasted. Fish and small game like hares and rabbits were cooked in hanging grills – hinged grids between which the meat was sandwiched before being hooked over the firebars at the front of the grate.

Smaller pieces still were cooked on the larkspit, so-called for the 18th-century habit of roasting small songbirds. These stood in front of the fire on three legs and meat was impaled on wicked forward-pointing spikes.

Succulent smells of roasting meat were by no

▲ *Innovative barrel churns made butter-making easier. Salt water rinses prevented sticking.*

bred and kept to run the treadmill and provide the motive power for the spit) and the ingle beam itself was pitted with holes where mechanical spit-jacks were once fitted.

The more contained heat of coal fires required a

▶ *At harvest time, families of hop pickers often helped on the farm, staying up to four weeks.*

▼ *Pattens were wooden shoes set on metal stands, which raised them from the floor, keeping the feet dry whilst scrubbing floors or working in the dairy.*

means familiar in all farmhouses. Meat was a rarity in poorer households where the great staple was bread. The weekly bake encompassed pies, biscuits and cakes as well as bread, and was a major undertaking, exemplified by the large trough of elm set near the fireplace where the dough was worked and left to prove; there were also special moulding boards for shaping the loaves and bolting tubs for sifting out the bran from the flour.

The bread oven was near the fire, built into the great brick chimney with a small metal door. Known as a beehive oven after its domed shape, it was filled with brushwood and faggots and then lit with an ember from the fire. The door was closed for the fire to burn down, the glowing embers were spread inside to ensure an even heat, and then the ashes were raked out. The oven retained heat for as long as twenty-four hours.

The bread went in first, when the oven was at its hottest, manoeuvred in and out with a wooden paddle called a peel. One farmer remembered, 'If the oven was not hot enough the bread would be heavy, or "sad"; but we had to make the best of it.' The pies, cakes and biscuits that went in after the bread were, however, a great treat for the household. They were meant to last the week but rarely did so when there were eager, growing children around. Once the bake was over, and the whole kitchen was wreathed with the rich, yeasty smells of new-baked bread, the remaining heat was used to dry herbs, feathers for pillows, and sometimes clothes on washday.

### THE FARMHOUSE DAIRY

Butter and cheese were made in the cool of the dairy, a small room kept spotlessly clean – a speck of dirt could sour cream or turn butter to cheese. The small north-facing window was covered with gauze to keep out flies and switches of elder were hung from the ceiling to dry.

The farmer's wife usually looked after the dairy, although more prosperous farmers could sometimes afford to employ a dairymaid. The milk was put into wide, shallow slipware bowls to cool; the cream was then skimmed off and hand-churned to separate the butter and buttermilk. Finally, the butter had to be salted, laid to drain on a rush mat, then patted and pressed to remove any air or excess moisture and put into wooden bowls. Butter intended for sale was impressed with a carved wooden stamp made of sycamore or beech. Sycamore was also used for the butter tubs and churns, while willow was used for the churn paddles.

Cheese-making was another important farmhouse activity. Milk was heated and rennet added before it was poured into tubs to curdle. The curds were wrapped in muslin and put in a chessart, a wooden bucket with a ledge halfway down. The cheese was weighted with a heavy stone, thus allowing the whey to drain off through holes in the ledge. Cheeses and butter both needed cool conditions to keep and the dairy was always kept cool, with slate and polished stone surfaces.

The dairy roof was either thatched or tiled with stone, and was sometimes built under the shade of trees to insulate the room from the heat of the sun.

## LIFE AND LEISURE

# Hop Picking

HOP PICKING AND BEER MAKING WAS AN INTEGRAL PART OF FARM LIFE, PARTICULARLY IN THE SOUTH OF ENGLAND. HARVESTING TOOK PLACE IN AUGUST AND PROVIDED WELCOME WORK FOR HUNDREDS OF WORKERS LIVING IN LARGER TOWNS. THE AVERAGE WAGE WAS TEN SHILLINGS A WEEK, AND THE MORE FORTUNATE LABOURERS MIGHT EXPECT A FREE MEAL AND A READY SUPPLY OF ALE IN EXCHANGE FOR THEIR EFFORTS. ONCE PICKED, THE HOPS WERE GATHERED UP AND PUT INTO LARGE SACKS WHICH WERE HUNG TO DRY. SAMPLING EQUIPMENT WAS USED TO SELECT THE HOPS FOR BREWING, EITHER ON THE FARM OR AT THE BREWERY.

▶ HOP SAMPLING UTENSILS WERE USED TO SEND A SAMPLE OF THE HARVEST TO THE LOCAL BREWERY. THE KNIFE CUT OPEN THE SACK AND THE HOPS WERE EXTRACTED WITH THE FORKS AND PRESSED IN THE BOX.

▲ BEER MUGS AND JUG, DECORATED WITH HOPS AND BARLEY C. 1860.

◀ *Wooden spoons, used for a variety of kitchen chores, were housed in a rack on the kitchen wall.*

# The Copper Kettle

Indispensable in the farmhouse kitchen, this bright,
durable but essentially humble article is now a prized
and much imitated collector's piece

Tea was the common denominator of Victorian society; from the castle to the cottage, it was a part of everybody's daily life. And with the cup of tea arrived its indispensable companion, the copper tea kettle – a piece of kitchen equipment superbly suited to its purpose. Far smaller than the cast iron or brass cooking ware that had hung over open fires since Roman times, the tea kettle was designed to boil quickly. Suspended from an elaborate chimney crane over an old-fashioned hearth or singing on the iron hob of a modern coal-fuelled grate, the kettle was both efficient and attractive. In the farmhouse kitchen – never empty, never still – the water would scarcely have begun to cool before the tea kettle would be set to boil again.

### DEVELOPMENT OF THE KETTLE

The design of the tea kettle was not a Victorian innovation. The Romans had boiled water in a similar type of vessel called an *aquamanile,* and spouted pots later reappeared in Europe during the Middle Ages. But cooking over a hot and unpredictable open fire did not promote the use of sophisticated equipment or techniques. If food was not turned on a spit it was generally simmered in a pot. For soups, stews, boiled joints or just plain hot water, the heavy cast metal cauldron was the workhouse of many country kitchens, and was still to

## Kettle with Burner

A BRASS AND COPPER KETTLE ON A PORTABLE
WROUGHT-IRON STAND. BENEATH IT IS A BRASS
AND COPPER SPIRIT BURNER TO HEAT THE WATER.

▼ *Sitting on a brass trivet, the copper kettle on the table has a round, movable handle, indicating an early 19th century design. The kettle on the dresser has a fixed handle with a wooden grip – features of later designs.*

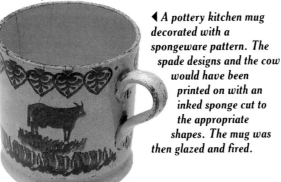

◄ *A pottery kitchen mug decorated with a spongeware pattern. The spade designs and the cow would have been printed on with an inked sponge cut to the appropriate shapes. The mug was then glazed and fired.*

## Kettle Designs

EDWARDIAN-STYLE COPPER KETTLE WITH A BRASS RIM AND A FIXED BRASS AND WOOD HANDLE.

A BELL-SHAPED VICTORIAN KETTLE WITH A MOVABLE HANDLE. THE BRASS SPOUT HAS BEEN SOLDERED TO THE BODY.

A LARGE KETTLE, PITTED FROM LONG USE. THE BODY AND SPOUT SHAPES ARE TYPICALLY VICTORIAN.

be found during the Victorian era. Its rounded base distributed the heat evenly as it hung over the fire or stood among the embers on its own short legs.

For a quick cup of tea, however, the cauldron was a bit of a dinosaur. Tea called for an easily-manageable container to boil a small amount of water as quickly as possible. To accomplish this, the *aquamanile* was rediscovered and quickly adapted as a tea kettle for the new national drink. Its serpentine spout permitted steam to escape without the kettle boiling over, and its flat bottom allowed it to be removed from the heat and put down without toppling over or – with new technology – brought to the boil on the flat top of a hob grate or kitchen range.

Kettles dating from the early 18th century, when tea was still a rich man's drink, were made of silver, a highly heat-conductive metal. As tea became a regular habit for the ordinary man, however, cheaper metals prevailed. Although some kettles were made of brass and iron, copper was the most successful material; bright and inexpensive it was second only to silver as an efficient conductor of heat. By Queen Victoria's reign, Britain was the world's principal producer of copper, as well as the principal western consumer of tea. In even the humblest cottage, a copper kettle was beside the fire.

### SHAPES AND STYLES

The word 'kettle' did not refer exclusively to tea in the 19th century. Round or oval ham and fish kettles – without spouts – were to be found in most kitchens. Nor were all tea kettles the same comforting shape we recognize today – the rounded shoulders, cylindrical body and angular spout, like the neck of an advancing goose. Some were oval, others flat-topped or pot-bellied. Among the most striking experiments were the low, square or rectangular models popular at the end of the 18th century. Known as fast-boiling kettles, these were intended to speed up the tea break by maximizing the metal surface that came in contact with the hob (a recent development in cooking). One particularly original variation was the half kettle, semi-circular in shape, its flat side designed to be placed against the grate. Unconventionally shaped kettles such as these were more difficult to repair than circular ones, a decided disadvantage in the days when kitchen utensils were expected to last.

The circular kettle survived relatively unchanged for over 200 years because there was simply nothing better. There were, of course, minor variations in the basic design. The metal handles of early 19th

*Copper kettles are decorative but old examples can be quite expensive. Those with a flat side would heat up on a trivet hanging from the grate. Cast-iron and brass trivets are often of intricate design.*

◀ *A large 19th-century, all-copper kettle of oval design with a solid fixed handle and typical serpentine spout.*

PRICE GUIDE ❹

▶ *Coffee arrived in England in the early 17th century, before tea. This spongeware pottery coffee pot dates from around 1860.*

PRICE GUIDE ❺

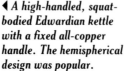

◀ *A high-handled, squat-bodied Edwardian kettle with a fixed all-copper handle. The hemispherical design was popular.*

PRICE GUIDE ❺

▶ *Another hemispherical Edwardian design with an unusual offset fixed handle. The lid has a spout for steam to escape.*

PRICE GUIDE ❹

century models, for instance, are often curved and movable; the straight-topped, fixed handle made of wood or bone suggests later Victorian manufacture.

Construction techniques also changed. Eighteenth-century sheet copper was hammered out by hand and has a thick, irregular texture compared to the machine-rolled metal of Victorian days. After 1850 most joints were soldered; earlier joining techniques involved folding over or dovetailing the seams and hammering them together.

By modern standards, the kettle was a durable utensil, but daily use over many years took its toll. Today, 18th-century examples are relatively hard to find. Although ornate silver or brass tea kettles mounted on spirit lamps were proudly brought into the drawing room from Georgian to Edwardian days, their plain copper cousins remained by the fire. Only in this century has the homely kitchen kettle been acknowledged as a work of folk art. A down-to-earth contemporary opinion was offered by Esther Hewlett (Copley) in *Cottage Comforts and Hints for Promoting Them*. 'The beauty of a copper kettle,' she told readers in 1825, 'is in its durability and brightness, not its shape.'

### THE KETTLE IN THE KITCHEN

In country districts, especially in areas where there was a plentiful supply of wood, food was prepared over an open fire until well into the 19th century. Where this was the case, the kettle might be placed on a trivet by the edge of the fire or suspended either from a simple bar or hook, or from a chimney crane mounted to the inner wall of the fireplace.

Some 18th-century cranes were surprisingly sophisticated devices, equipped with ratchets and hinges that permitted the cooking vessel to be moved in three planes: up and down, backwards and forwards, or sideways. Because a large kettle might be too heavy to lift, or because metal handles easily became too hot to touch, the kettle tilter or 'idle back' was developed. This device enabled the cook to pour water simply by pressing down a long lever

▲ *Shaped like a coffee pot, this stoneware jug is actually a tea pot. The strainer in the sparrow-beak lip gives it away.*

PRICE GUIDE **4**

▲ *Trivets kept kettles and other pots and pans warm in front of the fire. The one with legs is free-standing and is adjustable. The other, more common types hang from the bars of the fire grate.*

PRICE GUIDE **1 2**

◀ *The kettle was not confined to the kitchen or even the house. Come harvest time, when the men were working long hours in the field, supper might be prepared over an open fire outside and served with mugs of refreshing hot tea, fortifying the farmhands for another couple of hours of scything.*

connected to a double hook from which the kettle was suspended. A large iron kettle equipped with a tilter could hang above a fire more or less permanently, providing a household with all its hot water.

A major development in cooking technology occurred in the mid-18th century with the invention of the coal-fired hob grate. Its small central fire was flanked by built-in cast-iron boxes, which provided cooking surfaces for flat-bottomed vessels. This was ideal for relatively delicate utensils such as the copper tea kettle, which could live on the hob without overheating. Although the hob grate still included an open fire, it was only a short step to the development of the enclosed range, forerunner of today's all-in-one cooker.

Even with careful treatment, a tea kettle might eventually begin to leak at the seams. When this happened, it was carefully put aside until the tinker arrived on his regular round. As well as sharpening knives and scissors with his foot-driven grindstone, the early Victorian tinker was a valued craftsman, who could prolong the life of a cooking vessel with a neat patch or rivet.

When an old kettle was at last beyond repair, a new one could be purchased from a travelling hardware representative. Since many villages were without shops, regularly scheduled visits from tradesmen were essential in order to bring the amenities of town to the doorsteps of farms and cottages. Less expensive – and less durable – items might be purchased from an itinerant cheapjack, who would empty out his cartload of inexpensive crockery and cutlery on the village green and announce his arrival by shouting 'Come buy! Come buy!' Delivery of the tea itself, and other groceries local farmers could not

produce, arrived in the village by carrier's waggon once or twice a week.

## A NATION OF TEA DRINKERS

Tea, which had been introduced to England in the second half of the 17th century, was clearly a fashionable drink in 1711 when the essayist Addison wrote, 'All well-regulated families set apart an hour every morning for tea and bread and butter'. As its price steadily diminished, it became a drink for the poor as well. By the 1840s average consumption was more than 1½lbs (750g) a person per year, its availability having been increased by the opening up of the China trade in 1833. Simultaneously, the consumption of ale, Britain's other national drink, diminished as poor harvests and prohibitive corn laws drove up its price.

Tea was not taken entirely for its taste. In many country areas the supply of water was unclean, and boiling was the only sure means of purifying it. Nor was tea always from the Orient. Country 'teas', as they were called, had for years been traditional drinks and continued to be popular throughout the 19th century. Many of these were taken for their medicinal qualities. Catnip tea was good for sweating off fevers, while hyssop tea and blackcurrant tea eased chesty coughs. Raspberry tea reduced the pains of childbirth; an infusion of stinking valerian, on the other hand, induced abortion. Other popular country teas included mint, lime blossom, thyme, camomile and cowslip. There were also complicated herbal recipes for making imitation China or India tea. One called for a combination of hawthorn, sage, lemon balm, woodruff and blackcurrant leaves.

Whatever the infusion – English or oriental – the same copper kettle sang on the hob until finally displaced by electricity and stainless steel. In a remarkably short time since then the humble kettle has become a prized, and much imitated, collector's piece.

▶ *The ritual of putting the kettle on and making tea became immortalized in popular literature. This illustration is by Kate Greenaway from* Victorian Nursery Rhymes.

*Polly put the kettle on,*
*Polly put the kettle on,*
*Polly put the kettle on,*
*We'll all have tea.*
*Sukey take it off again,*
*Sukey take it off again,*
*Sukey take it off again,*
*They're all gone away.*

# Dairy Antiques

Objects used in old dairy farms and by country folk –
such as milking stools and pails, butter churns, moulds
and prints and cheese presses – make fascinating
collector's items today

The Victorian farm which aimed at self-sufficiency – and most did – sited its dairy next to the farmhouse on the cool north side. Ideally the dairy had at least three rooms, more if cheese was made and stored there, with a good water supply, fires, a boiler, a stone floor with a slight slope for drainage and walls lined with plenty of stone shelves. Mrs Beeton recommended slate or marble, but she was addressing the landed gentry, many of whom put much thought and money into building 'model' dairies – some, like the one designed by Prince Albert at Windsor, ornamented with beautiful Dutch tiles and extravagant china crockery.

The average farm dairy was a humbler affair, but it too had to be kept spotlessly clean. Slovenliness was soon found out; if the pails and crocks were not thoroughly washed out, if the butter had cow-hairs in it or if the cheese was too soft, the dairymaid responsible seldom got a second chance.

### LABOUR-INTENSIVE PRODUCTION
On the first page of the journal kept by a Herefordshire farmer's wife towards the end of the 18th century is the timeless lament: 'The butter was longe time cummin.'

Before the days of railway lines and refrigeration, all liquid milk that could not be sold in the immediate neighbourhood had to be processed quickly into butter or cheese. The traditional methods were very time-consuming and involved much laborious cleaning. Such tasks, however strenuous, naturally fell to women. On small farms, where butter might be made once or twice a week for sale at the local market, the farmer's wife could manage the work herself, but on farms with larger herds, one or

---

### COMPARISONS
## Butter Jars

BUTTER-MAKING JARS WERE MADE FOR
KITCHEN USE IN THE LATE 19TH AND
EARLY 20TH CENTURIES.

more dairymaids would have to be employed to help with the milking and cheese- and butter-making duties.

## NEW TOOLS, OLD WAYS

Although 19th-century inventors were continually devising new equipment for the dairy, on small farms change was slow. New designs of butter-churn were always appearing, but in parts of Britain the upright churn, in which a long plunger was 'dashed' up and down, was in use from the 16th century to the beginning of the 20th. These were originally coopered like a tapered barrel, but were latterly made also in earthenware.

For idle dairymaids there was the rocker

▲ *Dairying played an important part in Victorian farming and nearly all farms produced their own cheese. Large presses and vats were accommodated in a cheese room which faced north to keep it cool.*

◀ *The smaller items connected with 19th-century dairying are very collectable today. Apart from the variety of earthenware crocks and jugs, there is a wealth of surviving hand-carved wooden articles.*

churn, worked like a cradle, but more common were barrel churns. The earlier horizontal ones had slatted paddles inside, but in the late 19th century end-over-end churns without paddles were found to be more efficient. For smaller quantities of butter, there were box churns, some rectangular, other cylindrical like small barrel churns, and also, purely for domestic use, glass churns, some using the end-over-end principle, others with paddles.

The churned butter then had to be 'worked' to remove excess buttermilk. Traditionally this had been done by the cool hands of the dairymaid, but insistence on hygiene led to the greater use of wooden butter-presses and bat-shaped butter-beaters or butter-pats.

Cheese-making was even more conservative. Well-equipped dairies had a selection of tools for breaking up the curds, but when no one was looking, dairymaids would still plunge their arms in up to the elbows, as they had done in earlier less hygienic days. Equally down-to-earth were the methods of preparing rennet from the freshly-slaughtered calves' stomachs, although in the second half of the century ready-made rennet could be obtained quite easily.

## DEMAND FOR MILK

It was the liquid milk trade that saw the greatest changes during the Victorian era. Even though it was unusual to quaff a daily pint as people do today, demand for fresh milk in the cities was difficult to satisfy. In 1800 London was still supplied by suburban farms, an enterprising Mr West keeping 1,000 head of cattle in his fields around Islington. Milk churns were carried through the streets on horseback, by pony and trap or by the two-wheeled hand-drawn carriages later known as milk-perambulators. When, after 1860, the railways opened up the city markets, dealers based near convenient stations snapped up local milk supplies.

The great drawback with long-distance milk was keeping it cool, the only methods then in use being to stand it in cold water or to leave the churns in a stream. The last 25 years of the century saw the arrival of ingenious refrigerating machines which performed a rapid heat-exchange between warm milk and cold water. Science began to invade all aspects of dairying.

Pasteurization was becoming common, thermometers were used at every stage of production, 'lactoscopes' and 'butyrometers' measured the cream content of milk and new forms of power were harnessed to butter-churns and cheese-vats. Although the old methods lingered on into this century, the dairy as a small farm building was fast becoming the factory we know today, fitted with stainless steel, aluminium and glass.

# Butter-making Equipment

The butter-making process began with cream setting dishes. These were made of wood, particularly sycamore (which did not affect the taste of milk) and cream, glazed earthenware or metal. Once risen, the cream was lifted off with a skimmer (or fleeter), usually of perforated brass or tin, and poured into a churn ready for processing.

Collectors with limited space concentrate on the wooden implements used in working and shaping the butter: butter-boards, butter-beaters and the lighter boxwood scotch hands, grooved to 'scotch' the surface of the butter. Most attractive of all perhaps are the wooden moulds and prints with which butter for sale was decorated. Most English designs incorporated a rose, most Scottish ones a thistle; Welsh (and American) designs were more individualistic. Other collectable peripherals of butter-making include curlers, wooden scales, scoops and bowls also, from more recent times, butter crocks of commercial dairies, though these are rarer than the smaller, similar cream-pots.

▼ *This sturdy yellow-ware milk jug decorated with coloured straps is late 19th century and typical of many made by local country potteries for dairy and kitchen use.*

PRICE GUIDE 4

◀ *Hand-carved butter stamps were originally used to identify individual producers when the butter was sent to market. In Victorian England, farms came to use them simply for decoration. Designs ranged from flower patterns to birds and cows, and particular regional patterns such as this Scottish thistle became popular prints.*

PRICE GUIDE 4 5

▶ *Many households would have had a sycamore butter curler for making large curls of butter for the table.*

PRICE GUIDE 3

PRICE GUIDE

◄ *This late Victorian butter barrel would have been used for storing butter in the larder. It is made entirely of sycamore wood which did not taint the flavour.*

PRICE GUIDE ③

▼ *Setting dishes are found in either earthenware or tin and are characterized by a large lip which helped in skimming off the cream from the milk.*

PRICE GUIDE ④

▼ *The cream for butter-making was lifted off the milk using a skimmer or 'fleeter'. Most skimmers were made of tin, although handles could be of other metals. The smaller example below has an upward curling brass handle. The larger one, made of brass, copper and wood, is particularly fine and more unusual, and its higher value reflects this.*

PRICE GUIDE ③④

▶ *Along with the large butter stamps, wooden butter rollers were used to decorate butter with imprinted designs.*

PRICE GUIDE ④

▶ *Prettily shaped and decorated utensils, such as this carved butter scoop tend to be earlier in date than plainer items.*

PRICE GUIDE ③

◄ *Pat-like implements with serrated faces, known as scotch hands, were used for shaping butter into rolls and blocks.*

PRICE GUIDE ②

PRICE GUIDE

# Milk and Cheese-making Utensils

No collection of dairying equipment would be complete without churns, milking stools and a yoke. Even in the 19th century, pails were still frequently carried on old-fashioned wooden yokes. At the dairy the milk was strained through a 'syle dish' or milk sieve, then cooled and transferred to churns, from which the milkman ladled it out with pint and half-pint measures.

Milk for making cheese had to be heated before adding rennet. This was done in copper cheese kettles or newly designed vats with a jacket for hot or cold water or steam. When the curds formed they were stirred with a 'curd agitator', then cut up with multiple-bladed curd knives. After the whey had been drained off, the curds were sometimes ground up even smaller in a curd mill, before being placed in wooden or metal moulds. Hard cheeses then went for pressing. Early cheese-presses were cumbersome affairs involving weights and levers; later ones used screw-threads or springs. Finally, during its weeks or months of maturation, a cheese might be tested with a metal sampler.

▼ *Milk bottles were not widely used until after World War I. In the late 19th century, miniature tin churns were produced specially for household use.*

PRICE GUIDE ❸ ❹

▼ *Cylindrical cheese moulds in either metal or wood were used for the final stage of cheesemaking. The chopped curds were poured into moulds and a wooden block placed on top. Pressure on the curds expelled excess whey.*

PRICE GUIDE ❸

▲ *Cheese samplers were used for drawing out a section of the core for testing. Iron samplers are the most common with various shapes made to the same basic design. Also shown is an improvised sampler made from a lamb's bone.*

PRICE GUIDE ❷ ❸

▼ *Two late 19th-century milk churns and a large tin milk container. The milkman delivered from a giant churn on a pony and trap (or smaller perambulator), measuring out the milk using excise-stamped measures. The large brass churn bears the words 'Pure Milk' and is most likely to have been used for shop display rather than delivery purposes.*

PRICE GUIDE ❸ ❻

▼ *Milking stools were made in various shapes, with three or four legs (except in parts of Wiltshire, where they only had one).*

PRICE GUIDE ❹

▼ *Large wooden ladles served a number of purposes in the dairy. These examples are carved from solid elm.*

PRICE GUIDE ❸

**PRICE GUIDE**

▲ *Pails of milk were usually carried back from the field or yard (where milking took place) to the dairy with the help of a wooden yoke with adjustable chains.*

PRICE GUIDE ❹

▼ *This patterned cheese tressle would have formed the base of two cheese moulds. When pressure was applied, the whey ran off through the carved channels.*

PRICE GUIDE ❺

◀ *Milk was always poured from the pail to the churn through a strainer to pick up stray cow hairs.*

PRICE GUIDE ❸

▲ *Sixteen-quart counter pan made of earthenware with a hinged tin lid. Dating from the 19th century, it would have been used in a shop.*

PRICE GUIDE ❻

PRICE GUIDE

## Stool or Table?

THESE SIMILAR PIECES OF
FURNITURE HAD VERY DIFFERENT
FUNCTIONS IN THE DAIRY. ON THE
LEFT IS AN ORDINARY MILKING
STOOL, WHILE ON THE RIGHT IS A
CHEESE TABLE (SIGNIFICANTLY
TALLER AND LESS WORN) USED
FOR STANDING CHEESE MOULDS OR
UNMOULDED CHEESES.

Over the last two decades, the relentless raiding of Britain's old rubbish-dumps has turned up a good number of trophies for dairy enthusiasts, in particular late Victorian and Edwardian cream-pots and butter crocks (or tubs), tossed away by housewives with no notion of their future value, despite the delightful decoration and lettering used by the dairies.

Even more common, of course, are old milk-delivery churns, many of them eking out their days in novel employment, as umbrella stands or pots for daffodils on picturesque railway halts. The great majority, being relatively modern, are of no great value. In most cases, they can easily be assigned to their correct period, especially when they carry the name of a dairy and their manufacturer. A little research will reveal when these flourished.

### PROBLEM OF DATING

The great problem with dairy antiques, especially wooden ones, is dating. Should you happen to find, for example, an old pair of well-used butter-pats, there is no obvious way of knowing whether they are from

Somerset c.1840 or Sainsbury's c.1940. With experience you can often judge if wooden tools are hand-carved or mass-produced, but a wooden bowl, a pair of scotch hands or a butter-board may be so well-worn that even this is impossible to determine. In any case, as such objects were commonplace in city dairies, homes and shops, they are rarely relics of a vanished era of English country life.

### POPULAR BUYS

Butter moulds and prints, however, do come principally from small farms and dairies; also it is easier to recognize hand-carved examples. These factors and above all their small size and great variety make them immensely popular with collectors. Along with other small articles of dairying equipment, such as fleeters, scoops and bowls, they can be found in many antique shops.

When dealing with large dairy antiques from the 19th century you will have to undertake much lengthier research, before you can be sure what it is you have unearthed. Local folk and agricultural

## The Butter-Worker

FOR THE MODERN VICTORIAN DAIRY THERE WERE A NUMBER OF MECHANICAL APPLIANCES ON OFFER WHICH WERE AIMED AT EASING PRODUCTION. IN THE 1870S, AMERICAN INGENUITY CAME UP WITH THE 'BUTTER-WORKER'. THIS WAS A TROUGH-SHAPED TABLE TOP THAT SLOPED DOWN TO A DRAINING HOLE, WITH A FLUTED ROLLER WHICH WAS MOVED BACK AND FORTH WITH A HANDLE OVER NEWLY CHURNED BUTTER. THE DEVICE WAS USED TO SQUEEZE OUT EXCESS MOISTURE FROM THE BUTTER, A TASK WHICH HAD PREVIOUSLY EITHER BEEN PERFORMED BY THE DAIRY MAID'S BARE HANDS OR BY WOODEN BUTTER BEATERS.

① LIFT-OFF TROUGH MADE OF SCRUBBED SYCAMORE WOOD

② TROUGH SLOPES TO DRAINAGE HOLE TO RELEASE EXCESS WHEY

③ IRON HANDLE TURNED DEEPLY-GROOVED ROLLER OVER BUTTER

④ SMALL WHEELS TO HELP WOODEN FRAME MOVE ACROSS RUNNERS

◀ BOX CHURNS WERE USED BY COTTAGERS TO MAKE SMALL QUANTITIES OF BUTTER.

·CLOSE UP·

① BRASS FITMENTS

③ HAND-CARVED
HANDLE DECORATION

④ CARVED HOOK END
TO SPOON HANDLE

② DAIRY SCENE

① LATE VICTORIAN MILK CONTAINERS HAD
ATTRACTIVE BRASS FITMENTS

② TRANSFER-PRINTED DAIRY SCENES WERE
A TYPICAL DECORATION

③ HAND-CARVED LETTERING ON KNIFE
HANDLE DENOTES ITS USE

④ DAIRY LADLES OFTEN HAD HOOK
HANDLES FOR HANGING AFTER USE

⑤ MOST PRINTS ARE MADE OF SYCAMORE

⑤ BUTTER PRINT DETAIL

### MAKERS' MARKS

THE ORIGIN OF MANY 19TH-CENTURY
EARTHENWARE AND METAL ARTICLES CAN
BE TRACED WITH THE HELP OF A MAKER'S
MARK. OFTEN, MILK CONTAINERS
CARRIED STAMPED BRASS PLATES WHILE
EARTHENWARE ITEMS HAD BOTH MAKER'S
AND SUPPLIER'S MARKS. THE BASE OF
THIS CREAM BOWL HAS THE COPELAND'S
STANDARD IMPRESSED MARK (1847
ONWARDS), A STYLE NUMBER AND THE
SUPPLIER'S PRINTED SYMBOL.

museums are very helpful in identifying farm equipment and deciding whether a piece conforms to the traditional patterns used in that part of Britain. They are also the place to see the best-preserved cheese-presses and butter-churns. If, for example, you were lucky to obtain a cylindrical container made of slats of elm with iron cooper's bands, with a close-fitting lid and holes in the bottom, you could be sure that your find was a mould for a single Gloucester cheese.

But unfortunately, it would still be very difficult to put a date on your treasure. The same would be true of milking stools, wooden pails and milkmaids' yokes. Of these somewhat larger items, only milking stools are commonly found for sale, mostly in antique shops that specialize in English country furniture. If tempted, you should be wary of dates optimistically ascribed to them by sellers.

### POINTS TO WATCH

■ Get to know your woods; it is useful if you can recognize the grain of woods used by country carpenters for dairy equipment: elm, oak, sycamore and chestnut.

■ A wooden piece is more valuable if it has not darkened too much with age, though, obviously, this would be too much to hope for in the case of a wooden milking pail or cream setting dish.

■ Avoid pieces that have been varnished; the essence of dairy equipment ought to be its freshly-scrubbed or authentic, time worn appearance.

▲ *Late 19th-century butter scoop.*

# The Rocking Chair

Comfortable and well crafted, the Victorian rocking chair was not only an essential item in the farmhouse kitchen but also an elegant addition to fashionable parlours

Among the most important items in the typical Victorian farmhouse kitchen was the rocking chair. It often stood in front of the hearth, always ready to gently lull the tired farmer to a well-earned rest after a hard day on the land, or to provide his wife with a comfortable and comforting seat on which to sew or, if she was lucky, just sit for a while.

A standard part of the repertoire of traditional country furniture, rocking chairs were originally derived from conventional country chairs, but eventually inspired a variety of different designs, from elegant bentwood rockers with upholstered seats to sturdy 'swing' rockers which rocked on a fixed base rather than directly on the floor.

## ORIGINS OF THE DESIGN

Although cradles fitted with rockers are well known from the Middle Ages, and were probably being used long before, rocking chairs do not seem to have been developed until the mid-18th century.

The earliest rocking chairs were probably designed for mothers to rock their babies with the minimum of effort while taking a rare rest themselves, but this is by no means certain, nor is the rocking chair's place of origin. Some authorities believe that the first rocking chairs, which appeared sometime in the 1760s, came from Lancashire, but others claim an American origin. Possibly they arose independently on both sides of the Atlantic.

The early English rockers were based on Windsor, spindleback or ladderback designs, the former usually having a typical curved wooden seat and the latter often with woven rush seats. Such designs were scarcely modified, apart from being simply fitted with 'bends' connecting the front and back feet, which converted the chair into a simple rocker.

## 19TH CENTURY STYLES

For many years the basic form of the English rocking chair, including the shape of the seat and the angle of the back, remained the same – until the Boston rocker appeared in America in the early 1800s and cheap examples were exported to England through-

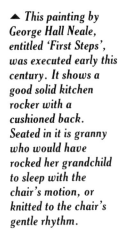

*▲ This painting by George Hall Neale, entitled 'First Steps', was executed early this century. It shows a good solid kitchen rocker with a cushioned back. Seated in it is granny who would have rocked her grandchild to sleep with the chair's motion, or knitted to the chair's gentle rhythm.*

*◄ A handsome hooped, stick-back rocker with turned finials. Owing something in its design to the popular Windsor chairs, it does not, however, have a saddle seat. Seat and back cushions would have made it a comfortable, good-looking addition to any kitchen.*

out the second half of the 19th century.

These were marketed in England from the 1860s onwards as 'Sinclair's American Common Sense Chairs'. The importers were at pains to point out their merits, not just in bringing rest and luxurious comfort, but also in their appeal to both gentlemen and ladies. Manners in Victorian England were far less relaxed than those in America, and women shared few items of furniture with men, but the rocking chair broke this barrier.

A further development came in the 1840s, when various English manufacturers tried to make a rocking chair that was less rigid and more resilient by fashioning it from cast iron. However, this proved too brittle to withstand the stresses and strains suffered by the bends, so more pliable frames were made from strips of steel or brass instead. These chairs had a single upholstered seat and back, and padded rests on the elbows of the arms.

Advertised as 'brass rocking or lounging chairs', one such successful design, manufactured by R. W. Winfield & Co. of Birmingham, was shown at the Great Exhibition of 1851. Later copies of these, using curved steel instead of brass strips,

with Thonet's conventional bentwood chairs, immediately took to his attractive and elegant rockers and by the 1880s they had become an accepted and popular item of furniture in English parlours and drawing rooms. However, although they were exported to America, they could never compete with the traditional Boston and other American types.

### SWING ROCKERS

The last radical change in rocking chair design was introduced to Britain towards the end of the 19th century. Known as the swing rocker, or platform rocker, it was described as having an 'action different to that of any other chair on the market', a justifiable claim, since the chair rocked on a heavy, fixed base. The 'Sanspareil' swing rocker, exhibited by the Scottish manufacturers H. and A. G. Alexander and Co. Ltd. at the 1897 International Furnishing Trades Exhibition in London, featured a 'silent, smooth and pleasant' rocking action. But it was in America, where it was first developed, in the 1870s, that the swing rocker became most popular.

were advertised as 'digestive chairs', recommended by a certain Dr Calvert as ideally suited to invalids – and ladies.

As this type of chair was not patented, manufacturers freely copied it and marketed it in the United States, although this did not diminish the popularity of the native Boston rocker in any substantial way.

### THE BENTWOOD ROCKER

The most important departure from the traditional rocking chair design appeared in Britain during the 1860s, when the gifted Austrian furniture designer, Michael Thonet, introduced his elegant bentwood rockers which had the same basic 'S' shape as the metal-strip types. Their comfortably angled cane seats and backs, and the artistic sweeps of their curved timber underframing made them more stable and comfortable than any other rocker on the market.

The satisfying curves of the bentwood rockers, shaped in steam presses – in complete contrast to traditional joinery – were often ebonized, or finished in gold or various colours. The cane seat and back were sometimes replaced by buttoned upholstery.

Fashionable people, already familiar

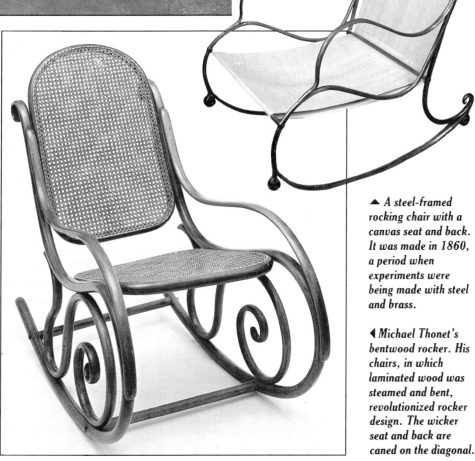

▲ *A steel-framed rocking chair with a canvas seat and back. It was made in 1860, a period when experiments were being made with steel and brass.*

◀ *Michael Thonet's bentwood rocker. His chairs, in which laminated wood was steamed and bent, revolutionized rocker design. The wicker seat and back are caned on the diagonal.*

◄ **DESIGN IN FOCUS** ►

# The American Rocker

THE SWING ROCKER, ALSO KNOWN AS THE PLAT-FORM ROCKER, WAS DEVELOPED IN THE UNITED STATES IN ABOUT 1870. IT WAS DESIGNED WITH ROCKERS THAT MOVED ON A STATIONARY BASE INSTEAD OF DIRECTLY ON THE FLOOR.

THIS NECESSITATED HEAVY UNDERFRAMING AND MADE THE BASE STRUCTURALLY COMPLEX COM-PARED WITH THE SIMPLE LINES OF THE BOSTON ROCKER. BUT BECAUSE OF THE STRONG SUPPORT THIS AFFORDED, THE SEATING PART OF THE CHAIR COULD BE MADE FROM LIGHTER MATERIALS, SUCH AS BAMBOO. EVEN SO, MANY MODELS HAD HEAVY UPPERPARTS TO MATCH THE BASE.

THE BACKS WERE INVARIABLY RECTANGULAR, NEVER CURVED, AND THE GENERAL STYLE OF THE UPPERPARTS OFTEN IMITATED 17TH CENTURY CHAIR DESIGN.

① SEAT, BACK, HEADREST AND ARMS ARE COVERED IN HARD-WEARING MATERIAL.

② SPARE TACKS IN THE WOODEN ARMS SHOW THAT THEY WERE ONCE UPHOLSTERED.

③ THE SPRING MECHANISM ALLOWS THE CHAIR TO ROCK ON ITS BASE.

④ SPINDLE STRETCHERS ARE TURNED.

⑤ CASTORS ON THE FRONT LEGS MAY BE MISSING, DAMAGED OR RUSTY.

## Spring Mechanism

THE ROCKER'S SPRING LINKS THE CHAIR TO ITS BASE. IT MAY BE RUSTY BUT A DROP OF OIL AND PERHAPS A RUB-DOWN WITH EMERY PAPER WILL PREVENT IT SQUEAKING AS THE CHAIR ROCKS. CHECK THAT THE SPRING IS FIRMLY SCREWED ON.

## Oak Rocker

A STURDY, STRAIGHTFORWARD OAK ROCKER, MADE IN THE 1700s IN A UTILITARIAN STYLE AND DESIGNED TO LAST.

Despite the popularity of the more fashionable curved metal and bent-wood designs, the rocking chair never really caught on in polite society in Victorian England. In America, where manners were more free and easy, it was always popular, and by the 19th century the rocker had become the national chair of the United States. Nearly every home boasted rocking chairs in the parlour and often on the back porch, too. It was con-sidered a compliment to offer a visiting stranger the rocker – if there was more than one, they were invited to relax in the best.

The first American rockers were made before the 13 Amer-ican colonies became the United States. The great statesman Benjamin Franklin has been credited with their invention, sometime between 1760 and 1770, when he was still a British subject.

### REGIONAL STYLES

There were several regional variations in America, including the Salem rocker, but the best known, and the one that became the standard American type, and remains so to this day, was the Boston rocker. Introduced early in the 19th century, its roll

seat and roll arms were in careful proportion to the curves of the 'bends', or rockers, mak-ing it exceptionally comfortable.

Apart from these refine-ments, the Boston rocker was basically a tall, comb-backed Windsor design. The comb piece was often decorated with an ornamental panel of stencilled or painted flower or fruit designs. Examples can also be found with railroad scenes on the comb piece. Later versions, manufactured towards the end of the 19th century, were far fancier, with dramatically taper-ing back rails, but still revealed their Windsor origins.

## ·PRICE GUIDE·

# Rocking Chairs

◀ A NURSING ROCKER, FROM AROUND 1820, IN SIMULATED BAMBOO WITH A LOW RUSH SEAT. IT HAS NEW RUNNERS.

PRICE GUIDE **5**

▲ AN EARLY 19TH-CENTURY, STAINED PINE ROCKER WITH A CURVED WOODEN SEAT AND CARVED SPINDLE BACK.

PRICE GUIDE **7**

◀ A PAINTED AND DECORATED AMERICAN BOSTON ROCKER WITH A ROLL SEAT.

PRICE GUIDE **6**

▲ A CHILD'S COMB-DESIGN, LADDER-BACK ROCKER WITH FINELY TURNED ARMS, UPRIGHTS AND STRETCHERS.

PRICE GUIDE **7**

▼ A COUNTRY CHIPPENDALE ROCKER WITH A RUSH SEAT AND CARVED SPLAT. JOINTS ARE SECURED BY WOODEN DOWELS.

PRICE GUIDE **6**

▲ AN UPHOLSTERED, BEECHWOOD ENGLISH SWING ROCKER WITH TURNED SPINDLES.

PRICE GUIDE **5**

Other types of American rocker were descended from traditional ladder-backed, rush-seated chairs. They had turned legs and stretchers, with their back posts topped by spike-shaped finials or knobs, and an upholstered panel or closely-woven canework filling in the high back instead of the original wooden rails. These were the type of chairs which were exported to England and sold as 'Sinclair's Common Sense Chairs'. In the importers' advertisements, much was made of the fact that they are 'found in every American home, and no family can keep house without them'.

### SHAKERS AND SWING

An American religious sect, the Shakers, were very influential in furniture design throughout the 19th century. Aiming for perfection, they produced strong, simple designs. Their rockers were made of hard maple and occasionally birch or cherry.

Their 1874 catalogue illustrated three styles of rocker – slat-back, upholstered and web-back chairs woven in 14 colour variations. Seats were usually of rush, cane, plaited straw or woven webbing.

Armless sewing-rockers had drawers to hold needlework equipment. Their lightweight bentwood rocker was distinguished from Thonet's designs by its simplicity.

In 1828 a new Shaker rocker sold for just two dollars and fifty cents.

Other manufacturers produced the complex and heavy swing rocker. This soon became popular, thanks to its particularly gentle and silent rocking motion, with no danger of the whole chair moving across the floor. Another great advantage was that it could be tilted backwards and kept at a comfortable angle for writing – or taking a quick nap. The design was so successful that it is still made today.

### POINTS TO WATCH

■ Examine the runners, or 'bends' of old rocking chairs; extensive signs of wear and smoothness indicate the genuine article.

■ On old bentwood rockers, taut panels are caned on the diagonal (never the horizontal or vertical) to allow for the 'springiness' of the chair.

■ Examine decorative panels on old Boston rockers; fakes may have modern, artificially faded designs.

■ Check the joints between legs and runners for cracks or missing dowels. Damage can often be successfully repaired.

# The Cottage Kitchen

Rustic simplicity combined with a bustling homeliness
made the typical Edwardian cottage kitchen the heart of
everyday family life

A casual observer could be forgiven for thinking that the Edwardian cottage kitchen hadn't changed for centuries. It was a mellow room, furnished with a functional simplicity that has become popular once again in modern-day homes. In reality, however, the room had evolved into a subtle blend of old with new. Alongside the traditional cooking paraphernalia, innovatory developments, such as running water and the ever-improving kitchen range, had made life easier.

With no servants to clean and prepare meals, the cottager and his family were naturally drawn to the kitchen, where there was a warmth and homeliness lacking in the rest of the house. The kitchen was the centre of all household activities and everyday chores. None of the Victorian clutter was found in this Edwardian living area, just the bare essentials — table, chairs and dresser — were required. A friendly fire and full bellies were the simple needs of the countryman's family.

*◄◄ The Edwardian cottage kitchen was at once practical and homely, being at the centre of family life throughout the day.*

*◄▼ Left, cottage kitchen implements were plain and functional. Below, a modern kitchen can be given the Edwardian cottage treatment to create a warm, natural, welcoming atmosphere.*

The kitchen was the living room of the cottage. Here the family took their meals, did their washing and all the household chores. Then, after the day's work was done and the candles were lit, the housewife sat by the fire with her work-basket while her husband smoked his pipe, supped his ale and read the local newspaper, and the children played on the floor. Such was the importance of the kitchen in Edwardian cottages, and the poverty of the occupants, that in a labourer's home, the kitchen might have been the only room on the ground floor, with just a couple of bedrooms above.

### HEARTH AND HOME

On one side of the kitchen was the fireplace — the focal point of the room and the heart of the house. It provided the means for cooking and heating and a comfortable place to sit and work or relax. It required a good deal of attention, but served many purposes, as D. H. Lawrence's description of a miner's cottage in *Sons and Lovers* illustrates: 'He went downstairs in his shirt and then struggled into the pit-trousers, which were left on the hearth to warm all night. There was always a fire, because Mrs Morel raked. And the first sound in the house was the bang, bang of the poker against the raker, as Morel smashed the remainder of the coal to make the kettle, which was filled and left on the hob, finally boil ... then he got his breakfast, made the tea, packed the bottom of the doors with rugs to shut out the draught, piled a big fire, and sat down to an hour of joy.'

Few houses retained the old-fashioned open fire. Instead, most had a range standing in the fireplace recess. These ranges were solid-fuel burners although, in some areas, gas stoves were installed. Gas had first been used for cooking as early as the 1830s, but primitive designs and a distrust of this odorous fuel delayed its widespread use.

The range itself was a squat, rectangular stove made of cast iron, in either an open or a closed design. A typical open range of the period had a central fire with

▲ *Turn-of-the-century cottage cooking was noted for its simplicity. The wife became adept at imaginatively stretching her resources and supplementing meals with bread, pastry and potatoes. Typical fare might be porridge, fried eggs and bread for breakfast, pie or stew for lunch and bread and cheese for dinner.*

◀ *The welcome warmth from the fire and relatively cosy atmosphere of the kitchen was a great comfort to the cottager. A moment's peace meant resting awhile by the hearth with a book or some sewing.*

a hob grate. On the hob there was invariably a steaming iron kettle. On one or both sides of the grate was a brick-lined oven used for baking. Beside or behind the grate was a water tank, heated by the fire. Later on grates and fires were enclosed underneath a hot plate and shut in with a cast-iron door. These were called closed grates or kitcheners and proved much cleaner than their predecessors. Keeping the range going and cooking on it was hard work, but a competent cook could produce a wealth of dishes by skilful use of the hot plate and ovens. Indeed, the range could be more versatile than much of today's high-tech equipment.

Above the length of the fireplace was a wooden mantelpiece. Arranged along the top of this shelf were an assortment of the cottager's treasures: a wooden clock, ornamental brass kettle, toby jug and candlesticks. There might also be a selection of souvenir ornaments such as a coronation mug, as well as some china or glass picked up on a day trip to a local town or seaside resort. Containers of salt, together with tins of tea and biscuits were placed here, too, for convenience. Sometimes a strip of lace or material was tacked along the edge of the shelf for decoration.

Suspended around the fireplace were the fire implements and, occasionally, the cooking pans.

## COUNTRY CRAFTS

For the Edwardian cottager, the choice of furniture depended upon regional variations on the basic functional pieces — table, chairs and dresser. New articles made in traditional styles, often employing local materials and skills, mingled with hand-me-downs from earlier generations and some modern mass-produced furniture.

At the centre of the kitchen was the table. Made from scrubbed elm or pine, the table had to be large enough to work at and to eat around. The cottager's wife used the table for all her chores, from food preparation to ironing and children's lessons. At the head of the table was a wooden armchair, at which the man of the house customarily sat. With a high back and arm rests, this was probably in the popular Windsor style, which originated in the 18th century, but was mass produced throughout the country at this time. Around the table were a range of other country kitchen chairs, usually sturdily-built and long-lasting in the local regional style. Some kitchens also had a settle. This wood-panelled settee was usually carved and had a box seat with a hinged lid that was used for storage.

The kitchen dresser was an essential piece of cottage furniture. This was generally free-standing and held an assortment of the home's best dinner china along its shelves, together with cups hanging from hooks. Purchased from the local market or nearby town, this china was usually sturdy, ovenproof earthenware, often decorated with transfer prints of natural subjects — such as the famous Willow Pattern — in tones of blue and sepia.

Along the broad shelf of the dresser, above the drawers, ranged a collection of roughly made utilitarian items — dishes for baking, platters, pitchers and bowls. These were made in part-glazed terracotta and were either plain or decorated simply with contrasting, coloured clay slip. Among these everyday items there were often small hand-made pieces — jugs, dishes and pots — in traditional country patterns. Local potteries producing such wares flourished at this time, especially in the West Country, due not only to the revived interest in handcrafted pottery but also to a growing

▼ *A cast-iron grate, adorned with fresh or dried flowers and decorative tiles and chinaware, provides an attractive focal point in the modern kitchen. If it is in working order and the chimney is clear, a grate will provide a welcoming glow in winter too.*

## Feeding a Large Family

WITH HUNGRY MOUTHS TO FEED, THE FARM LABOURER RELIED ON THE SMALLHOLDING, ATTACHED TO HIS TIED COTTAGE. THIS YIELDED FRUIT, VEGETABLES AND HERBS, AND OFTEN HOUSED A PIG FOR MEAT, CHICKENS, AND SOMETIMES BEES.

KEEPING FOOD FROM SPOILING REQUIRED INGENUITY. THE AGE-OLD METHODS OF PRESERVATION — BOTTLING, PICKLING, SALTING AND SMOKING — WERE STILL IMPORTANT SKILLS. HAM AND HERBS WERE HUNG FROM THE CEILING TO CURE AND DRY, AWAY FROM VERMIN.

▲ FRESH VEGETABLES FROM THE KITCHEN GARDEN PROVIDED THE FAMILY WITH BASIC NUTRIENTS

◀ WATER, ALE AND FARM MILK WERE STORED IN PAILS AND PITCHERS

PURE MILK

tourist industry. The lower part of the dresser might have two deep drawers for cutlery, and two sizeable cupboards for pots and pans.

### THE KITCHEN SINK

During the day, much of the woman's work was centred around the kitchen sink. Here, she would prepare vegetables and food and wash dishes. The sink itself was made of white or brown stoneware, with a wooden draining board to one side and wooden cupboards underneath. More and more cottages at this time were equipped with running water from a cold water tap. However, supplies were by no means regular and often there was water for just a few hours a day. Other cottages only had a hand-pump in their kitchens, and many people still had to rely on the village pump or well. Once drawn, the water was stored in jugs or pitchers to settle the sediment before using.

In addition to the sink in the kitchen, there would have been a 'copper', housed in an outhouse or in the scullery — an anteroom attached to the kitchen. A copper was a tub used for washing clothes, which had a fire grate underneath for heating the water.

Drainage was practically nonexistent and dirty washing water was often just thrown out into the back yard. To stem the flood of filth, the Public Health Act of 1875, with its amendment in 1890, applied legislation specifically to rural districts. Such was the change that in 1902 a cottager remarked, 'We've got very partickler about smells now ...'

### CHANGING TIMES

Despite some improvement in country conditions, more and more farm labourers were finding themselves redundant and were forced to leave the country for work in the town. In addition to these, a great number of men were taken from their jobs to fight in World War I. Those labourers who were left working on the land continued to live in basic, functional cottages for many years. Only gradually were the so-called 'modern' appliances introduced and basic facilities such as gas and electricity remained unavailable in some remote areas. It was not until well after 1918 that the old life started changing.

▼ *All types of washing were carried out in the kitchen or scullery, where the only supply of water might be found. Here dishes were washed, often in a tub, and baths were taken. The laundry, however, was done in the copper which was usually in an outhouse.*

▲ *Blue and white transfer-printed pottery was mass-produced in factories all over England at the turn of the century. A technique that originated in England, patterns were mostly of Chinese derivation, such as the still popular Willow Pattern. Meat plates were displayed on dresser shelves in cottage kitchens, as they still are today.*

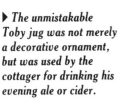

▶ *The unmistakable Toby jug was not merely a decorative ornament, but was used by the cottager for drinking his evening ale or cider.*

# Living by Candlelight

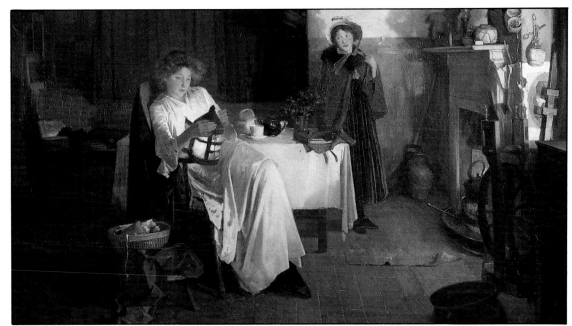

*◄▼ Candles in lanterns were useful in draughts and for illumination outside. The lighting of candles had only recently been simplified with the introduction of the safety match in 1889.*

In the first decade of the 20th century, candlelight, together with oil lamps, provided the main source of light in most houses in rural Britain. Coal gas, which had lit town houses for more than half a century, was relatively unknown in the country. It was not until the 1920s and 30s, when electricity became more commonly available, that candlelight was no longer used as a main source of domestic lighting. Even then, some areas were without electricity until the 1950s.

The candles used in the Edwardian country kitchen were those familar to us today. Compared to the ancient rush lights – made by drawing a rush through discarded cooking fat and still used in some remote areas at this time – the wax candles gave out a more powerful light. Even so, paraffin oil lamps were needed for close work, such as sewing or reading.

*▼ Candles were mass-produced and consisted of a wick of flat, braided cotton and fuel of paraffin wax.*

## Candle Accessories

IN THE COTTAGE KITCHEN, CANDLES, CANDLESTICKS OR THE SHORTER CANDLEHOLDERS, WERE ARRANGED AROUND THE ROOM. MOST WERE MADE OF BRASS, AND SOME OF WOOD, INEXPENSIVE CHINA, TINPLATE OR SPELTER — A CHEAP ZINC-BASED ALLOY. SNUFFERS, OFTEN SCISSOR-SHAPED, WERE USED TO EXTINGUISH THE CANDLES.

# The Biscuit Mould

Edwardian children delighted in sweet biscuits and
gingerbread. Using elaborately carved wooden moulds,
the mixture was formed into fancy figures and shapes
before baking

In the not so distant past, baking day was, like
washing day, a regular weekly event in many
homes. For children it was a day full of delight
and anticipation, for not only were there fragrant and
freshly baked loaves in the evening, but also delicious
biscuits, often moulded and shaped in wonderful
ways. Of these, by far the most popular types were
the spiced ginger biscuits known as gingerbread, and
buttery crumbly shortbread, both of which were
shaped in carved wooden moulds.

The day began with the stoking of the fire in the
kitchen range. Bread was usually baked first since
this needed a fairly fierce heat, and once the loaves
were in the oven the Edwardian housewife would set
about making the biscuits. For these she used a
fascinating range of implements – mixing bowls of
different sizes, rolling pins, wooden spoons, egg
whisks made from suitably shaped twigs and for the
biscuits, tin cutters and moulds decorated with a
wide variety of designs. The precious spices needed
to flavour the biscuit dough were stored in individual
drawers in a small spice cabinet.

Once the stiff mixture had been prepared, it was
cut into fancy shapes or pressed into wooden moulds
until a good impression had been made. The moulds
were removed, then the biscuits were placed in the
cooling oven to cook.

### THE ORIGINS OF THE MOULD
Decorating food, particularly sweet things, is an old
custom, and as far back as Tudor times patterned
rolling pins were used to emboss gingerbread which
was originally an uncooked mixture of breadcrumbs,
honey and spices. This was pressed into patterned
shapes, then left to harden in a cool oven. Spiced
biscuits remained popular and the intricate patterns
formed either by the straightforward rolling pins or

by carved wooden moulds, added to their charm.

By Edwardian times, the more refined cooking
ingredients and sophisticated kitchen ranges enabled
the housewife to produce finer biscuits than ever
before, but for the delightful shapes and patterns she
still relied on her carved wooden moulds.

Many of these moulds reveal a high degree of skill
in carving and design, particularly those made of
boxwood. Other hardwoods, including fruitwoods
such as pear, cherry and apple were also used.
Beech and elm yielded moulds for coarser biscuits.

### GINGERBREAD AND SHORTBREAD MOULDS
Gingerbread moulds were made in squares or
rectangles from wood cut on the end grain and were
generally between ½in (1.2cm) and 1¼in (3cm)
thick. Sometimes these 'cards' as they were known,
were carved on both sides with a random mixture of
unrelated designs which could be used separately.
Commercial bakers also used double-sided moulds
but these had a decorative pattern on one side and
the name of the maker on the other.

Shortbread moulds were almost as popular as
gingerbread moulds and, in fact, Scottish shortbread
is still frequently formed in wooden moulds decorated
with a thistle. American shortbread moulds have
Scottish emblems too, but these are often oblong with
distinctive cut-off corners and therefore easy to
distinguish from traditional Scottish moulds.

### MOULD MOTIFS
Gingerbread was a popular treat at fairs and fetes
from the Middle Ages onwards. Punch and Judy,
alone or together, were the most popular subjects and
moulds depicting them can still be found. Among
other interesting shapes were fairytale or nursery
rhyme characters, Biblical heroes, religious scenes

## Gingerbread Moulds

GINGERBREAD MOULDS WERE
CARVED IN A SEEMINGLY
ENDLESS RANGE OF DESIGNS,
THE MOST POPULAR OF
WHICH WERE ANIMALS AND
FIGURES. NURSERY RHYME
AND FAIRY TALE CHARACTERS
WERE SPECIAL FAVOURITES
WITH CHILDREN, ESPECIALLY
THOSE BOUGHT AT
TRAVELLING FAIRS, AS THE
GINGERBREAD SHAPES WERE
OFTEN GILDED WITH A THIN
LAYER OF EDIBLE GOLD LEAF.

▲▶ POPULAR ANIMALS
INCLUDED DOMESTIC
BREEDS LIKE DONKEYS,
HORSES AND SHEEP, AS
WELL AS MORE EXOTIC
SPECIES.
◀ MOULDS CARVED WITH
FIGURES OFTEN DEPICTED
EVERYDAY SCENES FROM
COUNTRY LIFE.

◀ *Baking was a weekly ritual in cottage homes throughout the country. After the family's bread was cooked, spiced and sugared biscuit dough was cut or pressed into pleasing shapes, then placed in the cooling oven to cook. Biscuit making was an activity which involved all the family, and even the youngest members could mix, roll and cut the dough as capably as any adult.*

▼ *As a special treat, Edwardian children could visit the local baker, who often displayed a mouthwatering range of shop-baked cakes and biscuits. Those with a few pennies to spend could choose between gingerbread, shortbread, macaroons, coconut cake and raspberry buns and other tempting sweets.*

such as the Crucifixion or images of the saints and historical characters. Others were based on traditional country motifs of flowers, animals and birds. Men and women in contemporary costume were also common and this can help to date the moulds. One of the most charming mould designs is the alphabet type; these biscuits were often gilded and given to children as an enticement to learn to read.

## BISCUIT CUTTERS

Although the traditional wooden moulds remained in use and are still made today, 19th century mass production popularized the tin cutter. Shapes ranged from simple circles with a serrated edge to more elaborate outlines. The heart was particularly popular but birds, stars, pigs and deer, initials, clowns, Santa Claus and, of course the gingerbread man were also favourites with children and adults alike.

In the late 19th century and in Edwardian times,

## *Confectioners' Moulds*

BISCUIT MOULDS ARE SOMETIMES CONFUSED WITH CONFECTIONERS' MOULDS, WHICH WERE USED TO SHAPE SUGAR AND MARZIPAN SLABS.

CONFECTIONERS' MOULDS DISPLAY ELABORATELY CARVED PATTERNS, OFTEN USED TO SHAPE THE ICING ON WEDDING CAKES.

# Traditional Baking

ALTHOUGH GINGERBREAD TODAY IS NO LONGER MADE IN THE UNCOOKED STYLE WHICH USED BREADCRUMBS MIXED WITH HONEY, MANY MODERN RECIPES STILL EMPLOY TRADITIONAL INGREDIENTS. THESE GINGERBREAD MEN ARE RICH, DARK AND TREACLY AND KEEP FOR DAYS IN A SEALED CONTAINER.

| | |
|---|---|
| 125g brown sugar | ginger |
| 1tsp black treacle | 90g butter |
| 1tsp ground | 1½ tsp baking |
| cinnamon | powder |
| Pinch of mixed | 500g sifted flour |
| spice | salt |
| 1tsp ground | 1 egg, beaten |

*Slowly dissolve the sugar, treacle, spices and butter in a heavy-based pan and bring them to the boil. Allow to cool, then mix in the baking powder. Place the flour in a bowl with a pinch of salt and make a well in the centre. Pour in the syrup mixture and the beaten egg then stir them together. Turn out onto a floured pastry board, knead well, then wrap in greaseproof paper and refrigerate for about 30 minutes.*

*Remove the dough and roll out to ⅛in (3mm) thick, then using a shaped cutter stamp out the gingerbread men. Place on greased baking sheets, then bake in a preheated oven (170°C, 325°F or Mark 3) for 8 to 10 minutes. Remove, then cool on a rack. Decorate with glacé icing.*

almost every household had sets of cutters (with plain and fluted edges) known as cutlet patterns. These came in different sizes and were packed one inside the other. Tiny cutters used for petit fours were packed one dozen to a tin. One of the most decorative of utensils was the pastry jigger – a small, jagged edge wheel fixed to a handle made from bone, tin, brass or wood. These were used to cut fancy shapes from the rolled dough.

### CONFECTIONERS' AND PLASTER MOULDS

Wooden moulds similar to gingerbread and biscuit moulds were also used by cooks to shape sugar or marzipan into elaborate designs which were added to cakes as decoration. It is not always easy to tell the difference between biscuit and confectioners' moulds, although generally sugar moulds had fairly complex designs and were more intricately carved.

Decorators' moulds for casting plaster shapes are also often confused with food moulds, although in general these are thicker and are frequently backed by another board. Collectors should be wary of such moulds which have the backing removed and the screw holes filled in. The subjects are usually cats, dogs and other undatable designs and the boards are frequently burnt to simulate age. Moulds were only used to shape the biscuits prior to baking and never put in the oven so this establishes a fake immediately.

### THE DECLINE OF HOME BAKING

Despite the Edwardians' love of the home-baked biscuit, its rival, the commercial biscuit, was beginning to take precedence on the Sunday tea table. Companies such as Peak Freans had been producing biscuits on a large scale since the 1850s, and new manufacturing techniques coupled with innovative recipes made them strong competition, and not only were they tasty, but they were cheap too.

The forward-thinking biscuit companies, always keen to increase their sales, took advantage of the improvements in communications provided by the roads and railways. New motorized delivery vans bearing the gaily painted livery of their particular company became a familiar sight on the roads, even in country areas, where biscuits were delivered to the most out-of-the-way grocer.

An added incentive to buy was the packaging. Before the days of airtight plastic, biscuits were stored in tins, which were usually decorated with lively and brightly coloured designs. Huntley and Palmer led the field in attractive containers, producing a great number of decorative tins in novelty shapes. Commemorative designs were also popular, particularly those featuring a royal event. These tins survive today in quite large numbers, although the more decorative designs are now becoming increasingly collectable.

With the quality and variety of biscuits available today, few people ever take time to bake at home, despite the enormous range of ingredients and improved equipment. Today's children may be familiar with the fairy tale of the little gingerbread man, but sadly few have ever smelt or tasted the old fashioned gingerbread from which the man was shaped in the story.

▼ *Birthday parties required special preparations, and on the eve of the day the home was filled with rich baking smells while all the family's favourite cakes and biscuits were prepared. Then, as now, the special cake was topped with a lighted candle.*

◀ *Yorkshire funeral biscuit mould with heart design. Biscuits were sometimes distributed in villages as a funeral invitation.*

PRICE GUIDE ❸

▼ *Egg whisk made from a naturally shaped twig – the forerunner of today's balloon and spiral bound whisks.*

PRICE GUIDE ❶

▶ *Earthenware salt pig with hand hole. Mid brown lead glaze with traditional Sunderland white slip decoration.*

PRICE GUIDE ❸

 ·PRICE GUIDE· ⟩ **BAKING EQUIPMENT**

*The equipment and containers used for baking and storing biscuits at the turn of the century can be found on sale and is called* kitchenalia. *Some items have changed little, and modern versions are available today; others are rather odd and their use is not obvious at first glance.*

Aubrey Dewar

▲ *Attractively patterned and shaped commercial storage tins originally sold with biscuits and toffees.*

PRICE GUIDE ❶

◀ *Two gingerbread moulds carved with birds and fishes. The larger mould, with figures, was probably used for confectionery.*

PRICE GUIDE ❸

▶ *Wooden spice box in the form of a chest of drawers. For ginger, cloves, cinnamon, allspice, pepper and nutmeg.*

PRICE GUIDE ❸

# The Country Chair

The survival of traditional country chair styles, right
through the Edwardian times, was ensured by sturdy
and utilitarian designs

In Edwardian times, just as in any other previous time or century, cottage kitchen furniture needed to be simple, solid and functional. While the rich attempted to keep up with the latest furnishing fashions, the average rural kitchen contained furniture made to traditional country designs which had remained virtually unchanged through the centuries.

### LOCAL MATERIALS
Up until industrialization, the techniques and tools used for furniture-making had hardly altered for generations. Most furniture was produced by local craftsmen who made use of the surrounding forest and woodland with all its different types of trees. Oak, elm, sycamore, chestnut, beech and birch as well as fruit woods such as apple, pear and cherry were used.

Rush, where available, was used to form a thick and comfortable seat on some chair types. The rushes took a long time to prepare, since they had to be dried very

slowly so that they did not become brittle. Once ready for use, they were simply wound round the chair frame, interlocking in the centre. The woven rush seat became associated in particular with two styles of country chair, the spindle back and the ladder back. These date from the 17th and 18th centuries but became widely popular and can still be seen reproduced today.

By the mid 19th century, the furniture needs of the majority of city dwellers were supplied by large-scale factory production. The Industrial Revolution and the new machine age that it brought was in full swing, turning out great numbers of chairs at affordable prices. One large factory in High Wycombe, Buckinghamshire boasted 'a chair a minute', a far flung concept from the traditions of hand-crafted, locally made furniture. In rural areas, the country joiners continued their local trade just as they had for centuries, using nearby resources to build long-established styles.

There are two main reasons for the

▲ *For centuries, the inhabitants of rural areas were dependent on local craftsmen to make and mend their household furniture.*

general continuity of country furniture. First, because it was basically utilitarian and made for everyday use, there was very little reason for it to change. A cottager's kitchen was the heart of family activity and chairs needed to be solidly built, as well as both practical and comfortable. Secondly, the styles that survived often did so because the skills needed to produce them and the particular working practices involved were handed down over the centuries.

### THE WINDSOR CHAIR
One of the best known survivors is the popular Windsor chair with its characteristic saddle seat, hooped back and decoratively carved central splat. Its long life is largely attributed to the fact that the chairs were seldom made by a single individual but had always been produced by

a team of craftsmen. The traditional crafts used were specialized skills which involved making the various component parts of the chairs separately.

The spindles, legs and stretchers of the Windsor were produced by 'turners', some of whom actually went into the woodland clearings and set up temporary workshops (after the 19th century, these men were called 'bodgers'). The turned parts that they produced were then sent to a workshop where one man shaped the seats and another supplied any sawn parts that might be required. A 'bender' steamed the curved sections and finally a 'framer' put the various pieces together. There were, as the years went by, gradual developments in the basic design of the Windsor chair and also some variations, depending on the particular region in which it was made.

Windsor chairs came to be made in most parts of England and in some areas of Scotland, Wales and Ireland too. A great number of regional variations developed on the basic types. Particular chair shapes, carved decoration and the woods used all

▲ Still popular in today's kitchens, country chairs of various styles will always give an inviting period feel to a room.

◀ A Sussex chair with ebonized finish, made by the firm of William Morris & Co. and produced in large numbers after 1865.

▶ This rush-seated ash armchair, stained and polished, was designed by Arts and Crafts disciple Ernest Gimson.

▼ The style of this bobbin-turned armchair c.1904, designed by Ernest Gimson, dates back to the 17th century.

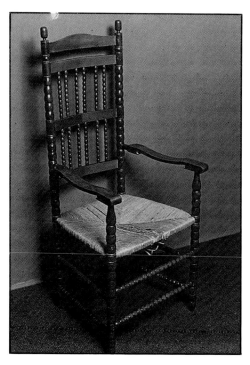

now provide clues as to the origin of individual country-made chairs.

### REGIONAL CHAIRS

As local furniture-making developed, there emerged across the country certain centres which became associated with definite styles. In Mendlesham, Suffolk, a variation of the Windsor evolved into a distinctive style of its own, and these chairs are now simply known as 'Mendlesham' or 'Suffolk' chairs. They have a lower, squarer back with arm rests, and the backs are decorated with rows of small wooden balls set between straight rails. Another low-backed variation of the Windsor which became widespread in the 19th century is the Smoker's bow, a

squat, solid-looking chair with saddle seat and heavily-turned legs.

Around Lancashire, ladder-back chairs, with their woven rush seats and curved horizontal slats, as well as spindle-backs, became popular from the 18th century. In Yorkshire, spindle-back and bobbin-turned chairs were made from about the same time. These later became a common sight in cottages and farmhouses throughout the country and, as for the Windsor chair, many regional variations developed as local craftsmen adapted the styles. Around the end of the 19th century and in the early 20th century, traditional country furniture provided new inspiration for designers such as William Morris and Ernest Gimson.

## DESIGN IN FOCUS

# The Rush-Seated Chair

In 1888, Ernest Gimson, a disciple of the Arts and Crafts Movement, produced a beautifully harmonious design for the rush-seated ladder back chair.

Gimson went on to produce a number of ladder back designs, all of which were notable for their lightness and elegance. Their tall backs generally contained five rails which increased in size towards the top, and which were smoothly curved to provide simple decoration.

The finished chairs were either stained black, painted or left as natural wood. A large number were subsequently made at Gimson's workshops in Sapperton, Gloucestershire.

① Plain-turned stiles tapered towards ends

② The rails, with exaggerated curved top decoration, increase in size towards the top

③ Curved armrest with smooth chamferred ends

④ Integral leg and armrest support tapered at either end

## The Spindle Back

An 18th century Lancashire spindle back with double rail of turned spindles

## Chair Backs

A Charles Voysey chair back in the Arts and Crafts style

Morris chair back in ebonized wood with radiating spindles

Rush-seated ladder- and spindle-back chairs have long been a mainstay of the traditional English country kitchen but towards the end of the 19th century these styles were adapted to make some of the finest and most sought after of country-style designer furniture.

In the 1860s, led by William Morris and the ideals of the Arts and Crafts Movement, a small number of architect-designers reacted against the dominance of mechanized production. They declared the age-old hand skills to be of far greater worth and began to design and make country-style furniture in keeping with principles of good craftsmanship and long-standing tradition.

In the late 19th and early 20th centuries, designers such as Ernest Gimson, William Morris and Charles Voysey specifically chose rush seating to complement many of their designs. Woven rush was a very old method of seating attached to a wooden frame without any tools, and had been in existence in England and Europe since early times.

### SIMPLICITY
The 'country' connotations of the rush seat were in perfect

THE CARVED SPLAT OF THIS
ROCKING CHAIR SHOWS THE
WINDSOR INFLUENCE

PRICE GUIDE ❻

A STANDARD KITCHEN CHAIR OF
MASS-PRODUCED TYPE, USUALLY
IN BEECH OR BIRCH

PRICE GUIDE ❸

LOW-BACKED 19TH CENTURY
WINDSOR WITH STANDARD
PIERCED SPLAT

PRICE GUIDE ❺

THE POPULAR SMOKER'S BOW
WITH SEMI-CIRCULAR BACK AND
SADDLE SEAT

PRICE GUIDE ❺

A LATE 19TH CENTURY YEW AND
FRUIT WOOD LADDER BACK WITH
CUPID'S BOW RAILS

PRICE GUIDE ❺

STICK-BACK KITCHEN CHAIR WITH
CARVED CENTRAL SPLAT AND
SADDLE SEAT

PRICE GUIDE ❸

harmony with the overall effect of simplicity the Arts and Crafts designers sought to create. While Voysey's chairs displayed a definite Art Nouveau influence, Gimson, in his chair designs at least, drew more on traditional styles. The bobbin-turned chair and his famous ladder-backs were inspired by 17th century country chairs. They were made by hand using traditional skills and tools but,

unlike standard country furniture, his chairs were sought-after by the most style-conscious buyers of the time.

### THE SUSSEX CHAIR
Gimson probably owned his interest in the revival of traditional rush country chairs to William Morris' previous examples, a range of Sussex chairs, also based on an original type. Morris' simple chairs had

first appeared around 1865 and were originally made in birch and stained black or dark green. They have lowish backs and a very distinctive arrangement of slender plain-turned stretchers and rails, as well as delicately splayed arms with curving arm-rests. Sussex chairs were made for many years, and Liberty's were still selling them at the turn of the century. They were also widely copied.

### REAL OR FAKE?

■ Modern rush-seated furniture and kitchen chairs tend to be made of pine. Older chairs were most often constructed out of elm or beech.

■ Standardized turning patterns suggest later mass production.

■ Saw marks on undersides of saddle seats suggest recent manufacture.

# Wicker Baskets

### The warm honeyed tones of traditional baskets, intricately woven by craftsmen using methods unaltered for hundreds of years, lend a country charm to almost any interior

In the days before industrial packaging and synthetic materials, wicker baskets were almost the sole means of gathering, storing and transporting goods. Small industries throughout the country supplied the demand, producing robust wares of all kinds for local use. Although never intended as decorative items, the natural materials and traditional shapes of the wicker baskets can make beautiful decorative features in both modern and old-style interiors today.

## A LITTLE-CHANGED CRAFT

The art of weaving has been traced by archeologists as far back as the Stone Age, and wicker had a multitude of uses in its early woven form, from hat making to house building. But the early weavers spent most of their working hours producing baskets for the fetching and carrying of food and fuel. Basket patterns evolved and were copied, until eventually the ideal shapes, sizes and weights were found.

The shapes and designs of the baskets have changed little since the early days of agriculture, as a robust and workable design was unlikely to be altered by fashion or whim. By the 15th century the industry was already well established in England, and in 1469 the Worshipful Company of Basket-makers of the City of London was formed. Growing, harvesting and weaving followed the same traditional patterns until the beginning of the 20th century, when the advent of World War I with all its social and industrial repercussions heralded the industry's decline. The Edwardian rural folk were among the last to work the land and make baskets in any

number. Whole families were involved in planting, tending and harvesting, which was often hard, back-breaking work.

Baskets were made primarily from willow which grew happily in osier beds on marshy damp land. The willow was planted in the spring and harvested in the autumn – huge groups of seasonal workers were employed throughout the country for the annual task of cutting, stripping, and preparing. Women and children took charge of the stripping, and in areas of the West Country schools closed for weeks to enable the locals to help with the harvest, which had to be finished by the end of the season.

## SHAPE AND WEAVE

The types of baskets produced by the basket weavers, or 'twiggies' as they were called, varied from region to region. Most workers produced baskets which were used for local industry – hop baskets in Kent, cheese baskets in Leicestershire and potato baskets in Lincolnshire. Coastal town workers made wares for thriving fishing industries, not only for storing and transporting fish, but for catching them too.

In some areas, baskets were woven from rushes, using quite different methods to those of the twiggies. The dried rushes were plaited together in strips, which were in turn sewn together in the form of a basket. Even with these softer baskets there was always the danger that soft fruit would bruise against the ridges of the base, but in 1851 Thomas Smith of Hurstmonceux devised a new form of basket which was quickly adopted for soft fruit picking. The

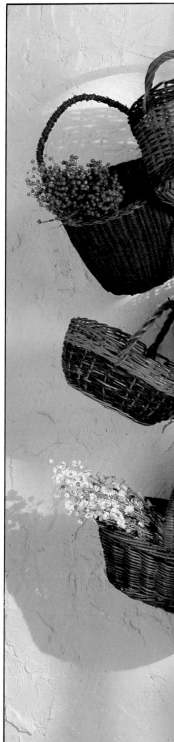

◄ *Wicker baskets and kitchen bygones look especially attractive grouped together and hung from the ceiling in the traditional manner. Dried hops and flowers set off the mellow golden tones of seasoned willow. Small baskets are ideal for storing garden produce such as apples and give the kitchen a country feel.*

◀ *Traditional baskets were made in an enormous variety of styles, each suited to a specific purpose. The shapes and sizes varied from region to region according to the needs of the local people who, in addition to ordinary produce baskets, needed baskets for planting, harvesting and transporting their crops.*

basket was made from willow cleavings which were fixed to a split ash or chestnut frame. This durable container became known as the Sussex trug, and was exhibited at the Great Exhibition where it caught the eye of Queen Victoria. A royal order was placed, and Smith set to work producing trugs for his special client. Once the order was ready, Smith set off for London on foot, distrusting the efficiency of the new railway system. He arrived at Buckingham Palace with his precious cargo, having covered over sixty miles, then promptly set off home again for Sussex. Trugs are still produced today using the same methods devised by Smith and his workers over 100 years ago.

Aside from the strong, durable work baskets, the

▶ *In past centuries, all fruit and vegetable crops – from huge potato fields and orchards to the cottage garden patch – were harvested by hand. In rural paintings, countryfolk are often depicted carrying or working with baskets used for this laborious task.*

◀ The baskets made for picking and gathering agricultural produce were each ideally suited to their individual tasks. Flower baskets were long and shallow, tapering to an almost flat end so as not to damage the flowers as they were placed inside. Egg baskets were round and large enough to carry two dozen eggs, and the fruit and vegetable baskets, which were oval in shape, frequently had a metal base.

willow was woven into many more domestic items. Picnic hampers, sandwich boxes, sewing baskets and even birdcages were familiar items in cottage homes and kitchens. Baskets were used for shopping, laundry and food storage – often hung from the ceiling to keep the food safe from rats and mice.

Many of the humble domestic baskets were in fact small works of art, different weaves and coloured willow creating attractive patterns. Many beautiful specimens were due to the twiggie's skilful work.

### OLD AND NEW

Today, plastics have to a large extent taken over from natural materials, and many containers which were once made from wicker are made in bright, wipe-clean synthetics. Much of the modern basketware available is imported from Taiwan, the Philippines and South American countries, although in small pockets around the country willow is still grown and baskets still produced by exactly the same methods used centuries ago.

The basketware found today in shops and fleamarkets is rarely of any great age, as baskets were practical items, originally intended to withstand hard use. Most suffered the ravages of toil and time and were eventually consigned to the dustbin. Some Victorian and Edwardian baskets can still be found, and these are worth seeking out, for their fine patina

charming details like buckles and leather straps.

Picnic baskets are among the most interesting finds, and sometimes they are sold with their original contents of china and cutlery intact. With a little patience, virtually all shapes and sizes can be found, from tall, thin wine bottle carriers (also used for picnics) to huge commercial laundry hampers which are ideal for storage. A collection of old baskets can always be supplemented with modern examples woven in the traditional fashion. These can look stunning grouped together and filled with plants and dried flowers.

# The Edwardian Laundry Room

The Edwardian laundry was a purely functional room,
decorated in the most basic way, designed to aid the
arduous task of the family wash

Newly built Edwardian homes often simply had a copper for boiling white linen built into a corner of the scullery, but many older, larger houses retained the Victorian laundry room with its high windows, stone flags and the essential pine table, which was often up to 14 ft (4.2 metres) long, for ironing and folding the linen. Some London houses had their laundry room in the basement along with the kitchen and other offices, although many found this an unsatisfactory arrangement. Some laundry rooms still had a box mangle for smoothing bed and table linen, which took up almost as much room, but most made do with the more modern and convenient combined wringer and mangle on an upright cast-iron frame. A lot of space was also needed to accommodate all the paraphernalia of washing – the assorted irons, drying frames, sticks for stirring the clothes, washboards and wicker baskets. Those who did not have the luxury of such space usually preferred to do their washing out of doors.

*A large laundry room was a necessity in a big household, and could be in almost constant use to ensure a steady supply of clean, fresh linen.*

Strange as it may seem, the most convenient position for a laundry room in Victorian and Edwardian times was right next to the coal supply. The advantage of having fuel to heat the water close at hand clearly outweighed the risk of getting coal dust over the freshly washed linen.

### THE LAUNDRY MAID

By Edwardian times, only the very rich could afford to employ a live-in laundry maid, and many families employed a woman, accompanied perhaps by her young daughter, on a daily basis, to do the bulk of the weekly wash. This might take just two days, one to wash and another to iron, but with a large family and bad weather it might take from first thing on Monday morning to Thursday evening before the task was completed.

The preparation for wash-day was time-consuming in itself; the fire under the copper had to be lit well in advance, as did the range if there was no other source of hot water, and the clothes had to be sorted into whites and coloureds and left to soak overnight in wooden trays or tubs.

In a large middle-class house standing in a good-sized garden on the outskirts of a town, the laundry room would be situated at the rear of the house, backing on to the kitchen and scullery. If the room was to serve its purpose well, it had to have its own water supply, and there would be two or three shallow sinks set against one of the internal walls to serve this purpose. The taps, in most cases, provided only cold water, but water could easily be heated up, as and when required, on the range, and, in any case, all the whites would be boiled in the copper. This might be of the old-fashioned kind, built into its own housing of brick in one corner of the room, or it

▲ The daily laundry maid was often accompanied to work by her children, as soon as they were strong enough to help with the scrubbing, wringing and ironing. Their task was not made easier by the fashions of the day, which included layers of delicate fabrics that all required careful handling.

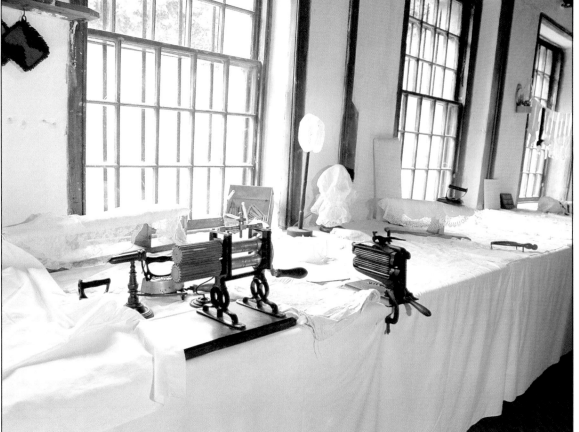

◀ The laundry rooms in great town houses had to be large enough to accommodate all the washing equipment needed for an efficient laundry. Much of this was in almost constant use, dealing with the household's clothes and linen, since the well-to-do were very particular about personal appearance and hygiene.

might be of the more up-to-date 'portable' variety. These could not realistically be carried about, however: the furnace underneath the huge galvanized cauldron had to be set on a brick hearth.

### SPARTAN DÉCOR

The floor of the room would be of stone, with good drainage, as there were constant spills as the washing tubs were shifted about. The walls and high ceiling were roughly whitewashed, the appearance of such a functional room being of little importance. Although the hearths would be brushed and the floor mopped

*▶ Simply carved wooden pegs were used indoors and out. On inclement days, clothes were hung up to dry close to the fire. But whenever the weather permitted they were hung outside for added freshness and a good airing.*

*▶ A brass soap dish would have been attached to the wall above the sink so that soap was always ready at hand for scrubbing dirty collars and cuffs.*

and scrubbed, cobwebs were often allowed to gather in high, inaccessible corners.

It was usually thought unnecessary to provide any permanent lighting, since the room was used chiefly in the daytime. On a dark winter's morning, a couple of oil lamps could be hung from the hooks or nails projecting from the walls (where the laundry baskets were hung when not in use), so that the housemaid could see to fill the copper, but the washing and ironing had to be done in daylight.

From the point of view of light, the best position in the room was taken up by the huge ironing table, which stood in front of the broad, high, shuttered window. The table was covered with a coarse woollen ironing blanket, and clean sheets of calico would be stretched over it while the ironing was in progress. Ironing boards in the familiar tapering shape we know today did exist, but were more commonly found in institutional or commercial laundries where there were a lot of skirts and petticoats to be ironed.

Many new inventions were available for the washing of clothes, as for the ironing, but these were generally eschewed in favour of more old-fashioned methods. The poor could not afford them and the rich had servants to do things properly – by hand.

## LIFE AND LEISURE

# *The Lever Brothers*

SUCH WAS THE PHENOMENAL SUCCESS OF SUNLIGHT SOAP THAT BY THE BEGINNING OF THE CENTURY LEVER BROTHERS, WHO HAD ONLY ENTERED THE SOAP BUSINESS IN 1885, WAS ALREADY A COMPANY WITH VAST MULTI-NATIONAL INTERESTS. THIS WAS DUE TO REMARKABLY MODERN ADVERTISING TECHNIQUES AND THE TIRELESS ENTERPRISE OF WILLIAM HESKETH LEVER. THE FIRM'S POPULARITY CONTINUED, DESPITE A HOSTILE ADVERTISING CAMPAIGN LED BY THE DAILY MAIL IN 1906 WHEN THEIR 16 OZ BAR OF SOAP WAS REDUCED TO WHAT WAS CONSIDERED A MEAGRE 15 OZ.

◆ A PACKET OF 'ROBIN' STARCH AND ONE OF THE MOST STRIKING 'SUNLIGHT SOAP' ADVERTISEMENTS. STARCHING WAS AN INTEGRAL PART OF THE WASHING PROCESS; MEN'S COLLARS AND CUFFS WERE BOILED IN STARCH POWDER.

◀ YOUNG WOMEN AT WORK IN THE LEVER FACTORY AT PORT SUNLIGHT, WHERE A MODEL VILLAGE WAS BUILT FOR THE WORKERS NEXT TO THE FACTORY.

Reasonably effective washing machines, albeit oper-ated manually by turning a handle, had been on the market throughout the reign of Queen Victoria, but these were still not regarded as a necessity.

The one piece of machinery that everyone agreed was indispensable was a wringer fitted with rubber rollers. Earlier wringers had wooden rollers which tended to damage buttons, hooks and eyes when they were left on the clothes. The machine most households chose was one that could be used for both wringing and mangling. This kind of wringer/mangle was still in common use in the 1950s, but by then the distinction between wringing and mangling had become somewhat blurred. Originally, mangling meant smoothing out the almost dry linen by passing it through rollers, a process which saved an enormous amount of ironing. If a sheet or tablecloth had dried too thoroughly it had be to sprinkled with water if the mangling was to be effective.

### A BRIGHT AND EARLY START

When the washerwoman and her daughter arrived at 6.30 or 7.00 on Monday morning, a certain amount of preparatory work would already have been done for them. The night before, the dirty linen would have been sorted into whites and coloureds by one of the housemaids and left to soak with a handful of soda in wooden washing trays, and the copper would be well on its way to boiling. The whites had to be washed before they were boiled, and to make sure they came out perfectly clean, the washerwoman would use her own knuckles, an old nailbrush, a washboard and soap, working away bent over a wooden tub.

The laundry invariably had a zinc dolly tub complete with a dolly peg. This curious wooden implement, which looked like a four-legged stool on the end of a long handle, was used for agitating the washing. The daughter might have worked with this for a little while, but would soon have been exhausted by her efforts. Even after this, the washerwoman would probably give each article a personal scrubbing and pounding; she had her reputation to think of after all.

▼ *The wicker laundry basket was an essential piece of equipment in the Edwardian laundry room, used for carrying piles of laundry out into the garden to be hung up to dry, and for storing linen waiting to be ironed.*

▶ *The weekly wash was probably the hardest of all household chores, and for the laundry maid it was often a struggle to complete the cycle of washing, rinsing, drying and ironing before there was another huge pile to be cleaned.*

The commercial brands of soap used in the Edwardian era were far kinder on the hands than the preparations used in the early years of Queen Victoria's reign, although the caustic soda they contained still left the hands red and raw. To boil the whites in the copper, the washerwoman added shavings of soap rather than the more expensive commercially produced soapflakes like Lux. Many articles like shirts and collars also had to be boiled with starch. When the whites had been boiled for at least an hour, during which time they had to be agitated with a stick (often simply an old broom handle), they would be fished out and thoroughly rinsed three times in a tub.

## THE BLUE RINSE

The final rinse was usually with blue cake, which was extensively used to disguise the inevitable yellowing of white linen and cotton. 'Many washer-women – charing women, notably – have an immense fondness for blue,' declared *The Housewife's Treasury*. One can hardly blame them; they naturally wanted their washing to appear as clean and bright as possible. The cake of blue, produced by firms like Reckitt's, was placed inside a small white flannel bag and put with the washing. The blue-bag, when not in use, hung on a nail over the sink, where it came in very handy for treating wasp and bee stings.

The speed with which the weekly wash could be finished depended very much on the weather. Clothes dried out of doors on the line obviously smelt much fresher than those dried indoors, but, if it rained, the clothes had to be arranged on tall clothes horses or a wooden drying frame that could be lowered from the ceiling by a rope over a pulley. However, a few grand Victorian houses had been built with their own drying rooms heated by hot-water pipes. By the 1930s the laundry room was almost redundant – in new houses with new appliances.

## LIFE AND LEISURE

# *The Apprentice Laundry Maid*

A LARGE NUMBER OF LAUNDRY MAIDS WERE YOUNG GIRLS FROM THE COUNTRY WHO TOOK SOME FORM OF TRAINING BEFORE STARTING THEIR FIRST JOB AWAY FROM HOME. EVEN AFTER SUCCESSFULLY COMPLETING A COURSE IN WHICH THEY PERFECTED ALL THE BASIC WASHING SKILLS, THEY OFTEN HAD TO COMPLETE TWO YEAR'S SERVICE WITHIN THE SAME HOUSEHOLD BEFORE THEY COULD BE CONSIDERED A QUALIFIED SERVANT. IN A LARGE HOUSE THE LAUNDRY MAIDS CAME UNDER THE CONTROL OF THE HEAD HOUSEMAID, WHO ALSO LOOKED AFTER THE PARLOUR MAIDS. AS MANY AS FOUR MAIDS MIGHT HAVE BEEN EMPLOYED FULL-TIME TO COPE WITH THE VAST AMOUNT OF CLOTHES AND LINEN TO BE WASHED EACH WEEK. HOWEVER, BY EDWARDIAN TIMES MANY GIRLS WERE BEING TEMPTED AWAY FROM SERVICE TO WORK IN FACTORIES AND SHOPS.

▶ DESPITE THE LONG HOURS AND ARDUOUS NATURE OF THE JOB, TO BE CONSIDERED A TRAINED LAUNDRY MAID WAS AN HONOUR FOR MANY GIRLS.

▼ THESE YOUNG GIRLS ARE LEARNING HOW TO USE A MANGLE AT THE ROYAL SCHOOL IN WOLVERHAMPTON.

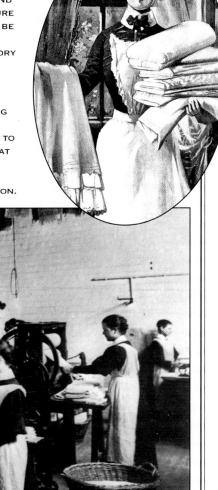

# The Flat Iron

No Edwardian laundress would have been content with
anything less than a battery of different irons to smooth
the creases from the delicate fabrics
entrusted to her care

Whether the washing was done at home in a purpose-built laundry room, was sent to a commercial establishment, or was carried out in a humble wash-house by a housewife toiling over a tub, every Edwardian household had at least one pair of flat irons. Outside the home, fashion specialists such as milliners and tailors had a range of irons, each one made to suit a particular task. Finishing touches would be added to a suit by the careful application of a lapel iron, for example, while the goose iron was used for pressing seams.

## FRILLS AND FURBELOWS

Edwardian dresses were covered with flounces, frills, and pleats. Lace cascaded down the corsage, and adorned hemlines and sleeves. For those who could not afford the real thing, there was the cheaper alternative of Irish crochet. Children's clothes were similarly decorated, and the taste for embellishment even extended to the nursery, where cradles and cots were adorned with layers of lace-trimmed muslin topped with satin bows. All this elegance required special attention, and delicate fabrics needed careful ironing and pressing.

The practice of smoothing or pressing clothes is generally credited to the Chinese, who adopted the idea in the 8th century, using a smoother which resembled a small saucepan. The Romans, however, used wooden presses to smooth out their togas before this date. Viking invaders introduced the notion of ironing to the British Isles in the 9th century. They used shaped stones which resembled mushrooms, with a central 'stem' for the handle. These stones

▼ *A view of the laundry room at Castle Ward in Ireland, showing how several flat irons could be heated at the same time on a large iron stove.*

*▼ Degas' painting of a woman ironing skilfully conveys the arduous nature of the work, and the physical exertion of the laundress as she leans upon the flat iron, intent upon smoothing the creases from the cloth.*

eventually evolved into the black glass smoothing balls or 'slickers' that were used until the 18th century. The Roman idea of wooden presses was also adopted in Northern Europe, where clothes were pressed by means of a roller and a board. Wooden linen slickers were used for ironing sheets.

Despite the name 'iron', early flat irons were made from various metals: the Dutch, for example, favoured brass. These irons were made by master craftsmen, and were often lavishly decorated with engraving. Humbler iron versions were made by blacksmiths, and some British irons were manufactured in cast steel.

### IRONS IN THE FIRE

It is unclear exactly when heated flat irons came into being. They may have been used as early as the middle of the 16th century, but the first written reference to them dates from the 17th century, and it was not until the 18th century that the first patent for a heated box iron was taken out by Isaac Wilkinson, a British manufacturer.

There were two types of early heated iron: the 'sad' iron (the name is a corruption of the word 'solid') and the box iron. Sad irons were heated by being stood on end on a special stove, or close to the coals of the fire. They generally came in pairs, one being used while the other was heated: when the first had cooled, the second was taken up. Care had to be taken when using them; the intense heat from the iron could scorch the fabric, and there was an irritating tendency for the iron to become coated with soot from the flames. Box irons, on the other hand, were much cleaner. They were hollow, and were heated by a red hot metal 'slug', heated in the fire, then removed with tongs and inserted into the body of the iron. The slug was safely retained by closing the hinged lid or door at the rear of the iron. Box irons were soon supplied with two slugs which were used in a similar manner to the pairs of sad irons. Box irons had more pointed ends than sad irons, making them ideal for inching into heavily gathered material or awkward corners. Additional smoothness was given to both types of iron by coating their bases with beeswax or soap.

### THE CHARCOAL IRON

Very few alterations were made to these two basic types of flat iron until the Industrial Revolution brought about changes in manufacture. The box iron was gradually superseded by the charcoal or ember iron. This had a body about 4 inches (10cm) deep, and a hollow interior which could be filled with red hot charcoal or embers. A row of holes at the side, and sometimes a chimney-like spout at the front, allowed any noxious fumes to escape. These holes, which were either triangular, clover-leaf or scroll-shaped, often made a decorative design. Some irons had a small aperture that could be opened or closed to increase or decrease the draught and thereby regulate the heat.

By the early 20th century, the Edwardian laundress had quite a wide range of irons to choose from, although the sad and box irons were still the most popular. The sad iron was made in a number of different sizes, ranging from 4-10 inches (10-25cm) in length and from 2½ to 4½ inches (6-

## *Irons*

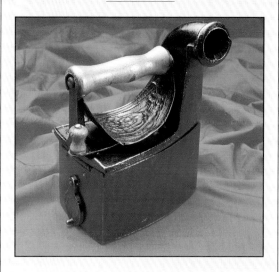

A LATE-VICTORIAN CHARCOAL IRON WITH A CIRCULAR DOOR FOR THE EMBERS, AND A SPOUT TO ALLOW FUMES TO ESCAPE.

AN EDWARDIAN GAS IRON, WHICH WOULD HAVE BEEN CONNECTED TO THE GAS SUPPLY BY A FLEXIBLE HOSE.

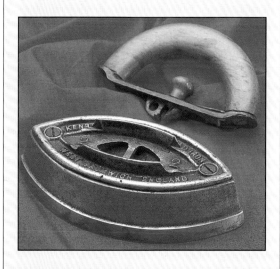

AN EDWARDIAN MRS POTTS IRON, MANUFACTURED BY A. KENRICK AND SONS. THE WOODEN HANDLE IS DETACHABLE.

▲ *This carefully posed photograph, taken at the Royal School in Wolverhampton in the 1890s, shows a group of girls being taught the correct way to use a flat iron. Their classmates in the background are learning how to operate a mangle and how to position linen on drying racks.*

11cm) in width. The irons were numbered from one to 12, and sometimes 14. This numbering was intended to give a guide to the weight of the iron, but as manufacturers did not standardize the numbers, they were not a reliable guide.

Perhaps the most notable sad iron was that patented by Mary Florence Potts in 1871. Known as 'Mrs Potts Patent' or 'Mrs Potts Cold-Handle Sad Iron' this had detachable handles that always remained cool, and a detachable base that was pointed at both ends. It proved so popular that it was manufactured under licence worldwide, and was

still being manufactured as late as the early 1950s.

Fuelled irons had first made their appearance in the late 19th century. Various substances were used: paraffin, petroleum, naphtha, alcohol and methylated spirits were popular in Britain and America, while the French favoured the use of vegetable oil. Running costs were relatively low: a spirit-heated iron could be fuelled for as little as a farthing an hour. The iron itself, which weighed 2lbs (900g), cost six shillings and threepence (32p) to buy, with the stand costing seven pence (3p) extra. Larger models were available, weighing up to 10lbs (4.5kg), and costing eight shillings and ten pence (44p), with a one shilling (5p) stand. Some were nickel-plated.

At around the turn of the century, coal-gas irons appeared. Some of these fed gas directly into the iron by means of a flexible pipe, so that an interior burner could be lit. An alternative was to place a hollow iron over a burning gas jet which was fixed to a stand. A variation was a German iron that operated on a rocking principle, allowing two irons to be heated alternately by a single jet.

Electric irons were first developed in about 1880. They were awkward and heavy to use, weighing about 6lb (2.7kg), and expensive to buy, as they cost about 22 shillings (£1.10). Many specialist irons were made to cope with a range of particular tasks.

·*PRICE GUIDE*· **EDWARDIAN IRONS**

*The most basic flat or sad irons can be picked up very cheaply at antique markets, but expect to pay more for specialist irons, or those with elaborate decoration.*

▶ *Edwardian mass-produced Italian or 'Tally' iron. These were usually sold with two heating pokers.*
PRICE GUIDE **5**

▶ *A fine brass and iron Edwardian goffering iron and poker, used for ironing ribbons and frills.*
PRICE GUIDE **5**

▲ *Flat iron with a detachable shoe, which prevented smuts from the iron staining clothes.*
PRICE GUIDE **2**

◀ *An Edwardian 'Sensible' iron made from wood and brass.*
PRICE GUIDE **4**

◀ *A small and simple flat iron manufactured by A. Kenrick and Sons of West Bromwich.*
PRICE GUIDE **3**

The tailor's goose iron was an elongated flat iron used for pressing seams, and so called because of the long handle that resembled the neck of a goose. The Italian or 'Tally' iron was a hollow metal cylinder set on a stand, and heated by a glowing poker. This iron came in different sizes and was used for the ironing of bows, ribbons, frills and ruffles. The fabric would be placed on to the standing iron and moved about. A variant, used for the pressing of mob caps, had a round body set on a stand.

### GOFFERING AND CRIMPING

Goffering and crimping irons were used for the ironing of ruffs and frills. The goffering machine had a number of ribbed, hollow tubes attached to a device similar to a small mangle. These tubes were heated by hot rods, and rotated by means of a handle. The goffering stack, on the other hand, used no heat. The fabric was simply threaded through narrow slats while still damp and a securing bar was then forced down and held in place with wedges. Goffering tongs resembled curling tongs but were applied to fabric rather than hair.

Milliners and hatters had various specially adapted irons. The hatter would use a rim iron when making a top hat, and the crown would be finished off by ironing with a nap-smoother. Both types of iron consisted of small oblong boxes with smaller slugs. They had extended rods, and the whole thing rather resembled a long-handled brush in shape. The milliner, who made ladies' hats, used a double-pointed iron that could be rotated in a circle for ironing the crown of a bonnet.

## Iron Stands

THREE-LEGGED IRON STANDS WERE MADE IN A VARIETY OF SHAPES AND STYLES. SOME WERE BEAUTIFULLY FASHIONED BRASS TRIVETS, OTHERS WERE COMMERCIALLY MANUFACTURED CAST-IRON PIECES.

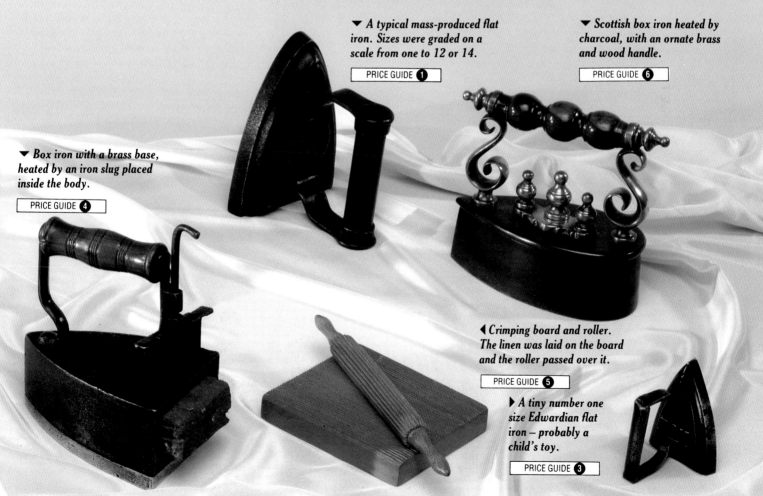

▼ *A typical mass-produced flat iron. Sizes were graded on a scale from one to 12 or 14.*

PRICE GUIDE **1**

▼ *Scottish box iron heated by charcoal, with an ornate brass and wood handle.*

PRICE GUIDE **6**

▼ *Box iron with a brass base, heated by an iron slug placed inside the body.*

PRICE GUIDE **4**

◀ *Crimping board and roller. The linen was laid on the board and the roller passed over it.*

PRICE GUIDE **5**

▶ *A tiny number one size Edwardian flat iron – probably a child's toy.*

PRICE GUIDE **3**

# Mangles and Washing Machines

While wash-day was still a chore in the Edwardian period, a variety of labour-saving machines had been invented to take at least some of the strain.

Washing clothes was always an onerous task, involving a great deal of hard work and disruption, and until well into the 19th century it was usually done without any mechanical aids. Until the end of the 19th century, larger, wealthier homes tended to wash their linen only once every four to six weeks, so limiting the havoc and expense that invariably attended laundry day.

However, a combination of developing technology and a shortage of servant labour meant that by the Edwardian period many homes had some basic form of 'washing machine' and most had a mangle or wringer for drying, smoothing and 'polishing' clothes.

### EARLY WASHING MACHINES

The process of agitating water, soap and clothes together was easy enough to achieve mechanically. The problem lay in doing it economically, and in a way which would not tangle or tear the clothes being washed.

The earliest mention of a washing machine comes in the diary of Dr Robert Hooke for 1677. In 1758 a book by William Bailey illustrated a complicated wooden triple tub machine and there were other inventions and patents sporadically through to the mid-19th century. Most were worked by hand and made from wood, though cast-iron constructions were introduced in the 19th century.

Machines generally worked on the self-explanatory rocking box principle, first patented late in the 18th century. It was a moot point which was more efficient – an experienced washerwoman with her dolly or the new-fangled machine.

In the 1850s, machines came on to the market which worked on the same lines as a butter churn. Thomas Bradford of Salford made one such machine, the Victress Vowel, which was the most popular

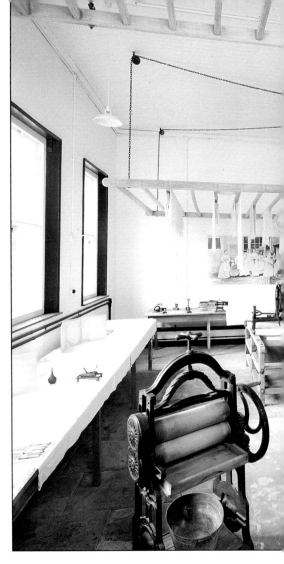

▲ *The laundry at Beningbrough in Yorkshire features a free-standing and a box mangle, as well as a battered wooden washing machine.*

machine in the late Victorian and Edwardian period and remained on sale until well into the 1920s.

However, none of these Victorian machines reached a mass market. Servants were reluctant to use them, and they were invariably very expensive. Before a viable popular machine could be made, two things had to happen. There had to be running hot and cold water available in ordinary houses and a compact power source had to be developed. Steam-powered machines were possible only in large country houses and commercial laundries.

### THE BOX MANGLE

Although the problem of mechanizing the task of washing clothes was proving intractable, the job of smoothing them and polishing them dry – mangling – which involved applying great pressure to the clothes, was accomplished by several ingenious machines.

The box mangle was invented in the late 17th century, the first true machine to be used on wash-day. This was a massive wooden frame, about 6 feet (2 metres) long, which contained a box filled with large stones for weight.

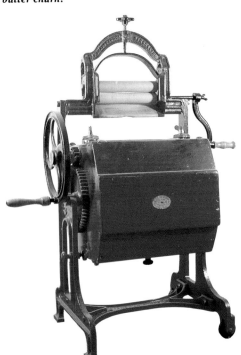

▼▶ *A pair of Victorian washing machines. On the right, from the 1880s, is a Morton's patent steam washer, with a crank handle to agitate the tub. On the left is Bradford's Vowel Y from 1897. The flywheel tumbles the whole tub like a butter churn.*

fitting so the rollers could be mounted above a tub, or a short, sturdy frame that could be set on a table.

The pressure of the wooden rollers, which were usually made of pine, beech or maple, was adjusted by a mechanism in the top of the frame, either involving a set of springs and a screw or a lever with adjustable weights. A large flywheel at right angles to the rollers provided the motive power. Although the earliest domestic mangles were set in plain, sturdy frames, they soon became much more decorative, with the name of the maker and the model often picked out in flowing script within heavily pierced iron panels.

Clothes were carefully wrapped around heavy wooden rollers, the smaller items folded inside sheets and tablecloths, and the rollers were set on a bed at the base of the mangle. A large flywheel at the side rolled the box backwards and forwards in the frame over the rollers. Sometimes it was geared, though not always, and a handyman often had to be called in on wash day to crank the big wheel. Although difficult to use, box mangles did their job very efficiently, producing bone-dry, crease-free linen with an attractive 'polish'.

Box mangles were the largest machines to be found in 18th-century country houses and professional laundries and were very expensive. As early as 1696 the Duchess of Hamilton paid the then vast sum of £53 for one. Large establishments and institutions continued to use them regularly until well into the 20th century.

### FREE-STANDING MANGLES
In the mid-19th century domestic mangles that could wring water from wet clothes and mangle damp linen were invented. Relatively cheap, they were instantly popular both for professional laundries and domestic use, especially in smaller houses.

The basic domestic mangle had two, sometimes three, white-wood rollers mounted in a cast iron frame about 4 feet (1.25 metres) high. Other variations had a

▲ *In the Edwardian period, the increasing shortage of servants combined with the ingenuity of British industry to produce a wide range of labour-saving devices. In this page from the 1907 edition of Mrs Beeton's* Book of Household Management, *a mangle features with a knife-cleaner, a coffee-roaster and a complicated bread slice.*

◄ *This Edwardian advertisement for the Safety mangle shows a lever system for the instant application and release of roller pressure and an unusual tubular frame construction rather than the standard cast iron.*

▶ *A copy of the oldest surviving mention of a washing machine, from Robert Hooke's diary for 1677. Strictly speaking, it is for a rinsing and wringing machine, attributed to Sir J. Hoskins, and it is unclear whether it was actually made. The description, and the illustration, is casually dropped into an account of the minutiae of 17th-century intellectual life in London.*

*Saturday, October 6th.*—Gave Bates and Hornes names for Sion colledge. with Crawley and Taylor at Jonathans, 15d. chocolatt. Directed them about Mr. Boyles chariot and my own with one wheel. To Mr. Godfrys, Dr. Whistlers, Mrs. Hewkes, Dr. Plot and Aubery. Saw at Dr. Plotts Rushes and the mud petrifyd to an Agate. Dr. Plot gave me his book. At Childs, Lord Elect. met Mercers Committee at home they viewd glasse and Lead pipe for the water and orderd them to be done. DH. Slept *p.p.* trying Sector tubes above with Crawley. Met Scowen at Garaways about Bonds, Sir J. Hoskins, Mr. Hill, we had much discourse about Royal Society. Sir J. Hoskins way of rinsing fine linnen in a whip

cord bag. fastened at one end and straind by a wheel and cylinder at the other. NB. whereby the finest linnen is washt wrung and not Hurt. Mr. Auberys picture by Cooper. Chocolat 1sh. much discourse about stables. Borrowd of Wyre, *Nouveaux Principes de Geometrie*—bought at a shop in Cheapside a French coppy book 4d.

# Free-standing Mangle

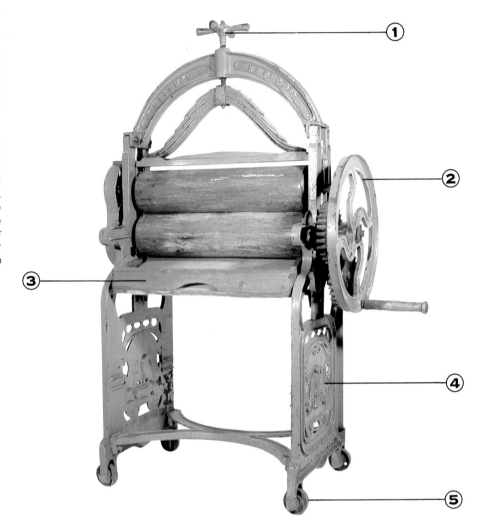

MADE IN RETFORD IN 1880, THIS MANGLE DOES NOT DIFFER SIGNIFICANTLY IN ITS DESIGN FROM THOSE MADE IN THE EDWARDIAN ERA. IT IS SUPPORTED ON A PIERCED CAST-IRON FRAME WITH AN X-STRETCHER CLOSE TO GROUND LEVEL. THE WEIGHT OF A MANGLE, AND THE FACT THAT IT OFTEN STOOD ON UNEVEN STONE FLOORS, MADE CASTORS IMPRACTICAL, SO IT IS MOUNTED ON FIXED WHEELS.

THE PRESSURE ON THE HEAVY WOODEN ROLLERS COULD BE ADJUSTED BY TURNING THE SCREW ON THE TOP OF THE MACHINE, CONTRACTING OR RELEASING THE LEAF SPRING. THE ROLLERS ARE TURNED BY MEANS OF A WAVY-SPOKED FLYWHEEL ATTACHED TO A RELATIVELY SOHPISTICATED THREE-COG GEARING SYSTEM. WASHING WAS FED INTO THE FRONT OF THE MACHINE. THE RUN-OFF TRAY BENEATH WAS TILTED FORWARD SO THAT THE WATER RAN AWAY WHILE THE MANGLED WASHING FELL AWAY AT THE REAR.

① PRESSURE ADJUSTMENT SCREW.

② FLY-WHEEL GEAR SYSTEM.

③ TILTED RUN-OFF TRAY.

④ HEAVY PIERCED CAST-IRON STAND.

⑤ FIXED WHEELS.

## Electric Washer

THE FIRST ELECTRIC WASHING MACHINES — THIS EWBANK DATES FROM 1923 — WERE MOTORIZED VERSIONS OF HAND-OPERATED MACHINES.

The early years of the 20th century saw a great increase in both the popularity and availability of labour-saving devices. The main impetus for change was the growth of the middle class and the decline in the number of servants.

Working in a factory paid better wages than domestic service. Even before the outbreak of World War I, it was difficult to get servants, especially for the many smaller urban houses that only needed a maid of all work.

Just as the relative cheapness and availability of servants had been one of the main obstacles in the way of the development of domestic appliances, so their disappearance from the job market acted as a positive spur to the development of more and more labour-saving devices for the home.

### EDWARDIAN WASHING MACHINES

Metal rather than wood was first used in the construction of washing machines in the early 20th century, though it was not until the 1920s that wooden machines disappeared. Galvanized iron was used for the tub and cast iron for the frame.

The rocking-box principle was still in use, but there were now rival mechanisms. One, produced by William Sellers of Keighley in the 1890s, used cogwheels to replicate the plunging, twisting motion of a dolly. Others employed paddle-shaped horizontal agitators.

Perhaps the simplest of all was the ridged roller which was mounted on the edge of a sink and pummelled out the dirt from wet clothes very much like a mechanized washboard.

The end of the 19th century saw a great growth in the population and wealth of the USA. Servants were very rare there, and people welcomed new technology. New ideas in washing machines, including the first electric washers, increasingly came from America.

The first electric washers were produced between 1906 and 1908 by the Thor Hurley Machine Co. of Chicago and the American engineer A. J. Fisher. Fisher's machine had an electric motor and belt drive on the side of the tub. Unfortunately this

# Mangles and Washing Machines

◀ PRESSURE IS ADJUSTED WITH A PAIR OF SCREWS ON THIS LATE VICTORIAN MANGLE.

PRICE GUIDE ⑤

▶ THE LIGHTWEIGHT FRAME AND FOLD-AWAY ROLLERS OF THE EWBANK REPUTE MADE IT SUITABLE FOR USE IN SMALL WASHROOMS.

PRICE GUIDE ⑤

▼ DESPITE THEIR NAME, TABLE-TOP MANGLES SAT ON DRAINING BOARDS. THIS EDWARDIAN EXAMPLE IS IN EXCELLENT CONDITION.

PRICE GUIDE ⑤

◀ A LATE VICTORIAN LEAF-SPRING MANGLE BY HENRY SPARROW OF BISHOP'S STORTFORD.

PRICE GUIDE ⑤

▲ EWBANK WERE A MAJOR MANUFACTURER OF WASHING MACHINES IN THE EDWARDIAN PERIOD. THE TOP HANDLE CHURNS THE WASHING IN THE TUB.

PRICE GUIDE ⑤

meant that the motor was soon swamped with water.

By 1914, however, the modern style of washing machine had evolved, with a motor fitted beneath the tub driving the agitator by means of a spindle through the base. A shaft-driven power take-off worked a wringer fitted to the top. For those households with no electricity, the Maytag Company of Iowa produced a petrol-driven version in 1914.

Whatever drove them – and Britain had no central electricity supply system, or grid, until the 1920s – powered washing machines remained a luxury item through the first two decades of the century, their cost of £30 - £50 putting them beyond the reach of all but the wealthiest

households. Even as late as 1948 just 3.4 per cent of British families owned a powered washing machine of any kind.

## EDWARDIAN MANGLES

The basic design of the mangle remained the same, though refinements of detail were made. Around 1900 it became possible to buy small wringers with rollers made of rubber rather than wood.

Rubber rollers were not so efficient at mangling, but had the distinct advantage that they did not crush and mangle buttons and buckles, a major drawback with wooden rollers inexpertly used. Later, the introduction of machines with a rubber strip in the centre of the top wooden roller combined the best

features of the two materials.

Edwardian manufacturers such as Ewbank produced ever fancier cast-iron frames but also recognized the increasing use of mangles in smaller houses. Neater and smaller models were made specifically for those working in cramped conditions. Table-mounted and tub-mounted models increased in popularity and some foldaway versions which converted into small tables were also produced.

Free-standing wringers and mangles could be bought from the larger ironmongers. In 1907 Selden & Co. of Hammersmith, London, advertised a combined wringer and mangle, mounted on a wooden washtub, for 90/- (£4.50). An iron-framed free-standing wringer was 37/6

(£1.88), plus an extra 5/- (25p) for lignum vitae rollers. Table-mounted wringers sold for 22/6 (£1.13).

## POINTS TO WATCH

■ If buying a mangle make sure that the rollers meet together and are not worn out.
■ Check that the screw mechanism regulating pressure is not jammed and that the springs have not rusted.
■ Working condition is always best but non-functional remains of early washing machines still have interest.
■ Contemporary ironmongers' catalogues illustrate the vast array of machines available and can sometimes be found in shops and on stalls dealing with ephemera.

# Washing Antiques

Laundry bygones are silent witnesses to a toilsome past,
when washing and laundering were the most strenuous
of all household tasks

S taggering about with quantities of sodden
clothing and cauldrons of water, their hands
reddened and wrinkled from constant immer-
sion in water, the Edwardian housewife, washerwoman and laundress managed the laundry without
male assistance. One reminder of what they endured
is embodied in the iron stands made from patten rings
that occasionally turn up in junk shops. Pattens were
traditional country overshoes set on rings, originally
developed to raise the wearer above muddy ground.
But they proved so useful in the waterlogged wash-
house that they soon became one of the trademarks of
the city laundress.

### UNCHANGING ROUTINES

The modern conveniences found in affluent and go-
ahead Edwardian households – piped hot water,
electricity and washing machines – were not available
to most people in Edwardian Britain. For the
majority of women, methods of washing clothes
changed remarkably little over several hundred
years. Right up to the 1950s, many did their
washing without the benefit of any mechanical
assistance apart from the upright mangle. Using the
washtub, the washboard and a few accessories,
generations of women followed essentially the same
routine of soaking, scrubbing and boiling, in an
unvarying cycle. 'The order of these should never be
changed,' warned *The Girl's Own Paper* in 1880,
'nor must the house-mistress ever permit the boiling to
precede the scrubbing, for the clothes should be clean
before being put into the copper.'

Even more primitive techniques, pre-dating soap
and hot water, lingered on into the 20th century.

▶ *Victorian and
Edwardian laundry bygones
can make a picturesque
addition to a kitchen
decorated in the rustic
styles, with whitewashed
walls and stone floors.
This display includes a pine
washing trough and stand,
a metal soap holder, a
galvanized steel dolly tub, a
pine dolly peg and three
plungers, or possers, with
metal cones.*

▼ *In the countryside,
washing could be spread
out in the fields or draped
over bushes to dry, so that
whites were bleached
naturally by the sun. But
this was hardly practical in
towns, where smoke, fumes
and lack of garden space
meant that washing was
often dried indoors.*

Lacking a really effective cleansing agent, women pounded their wet linen with stones or beat it with a club-like wooden object called a washing bat. Smoothing without the use of an iron was done with similar bats, some of them elaborately carved. These were pressed down firmly on to the clothes, which were wrapped around wooden rollers.

In parts of Scotland and Ireland, girls tucked up their petticoats and stood in tubs to trample the washing with their bare feet, scandalizing straight-laced observers; and in 1803 Dorothy Wordsworth, sister of the poet, observed 'a most indecent practice' – Scottish laundresses laying out clothing on the tombstones in a graveyard and beating it smooth.

As early as the 17th century most women employed some kind of bleaching or cleansing agent to make washing less laborious and more effective. Because soap was heavily taxed, lye was used as a total or partial substitute. This was made from wood ash, which was placed in the lye dropper, a special muslin-lined box with perforations in the bottom; water was strained through the box, to create an alkaline solution that loosened dirt and grease. But soap was kinder to linen as well as a more efficient way of removing dirt, and after the repeal of the taxes on it in 1853, its use became near-universal.

## A COMMUNAL RITUAL

Among ordinary people in the countryside, washing was a communal ritual for much of the 19th century. The village women trooped to the nearest stream or well, bringing a cauldron and building their own fire to do the job on the spot. This was never practical for town dwellers, many of whom had to heat their water in a cauldron over the fire or range. Some installed a boiler in a corner of the scullery or – if there was such a thing on the premises – in the wash-house. This kind of boiler was called a 'copper' even when it was made of other metals. Bricked around and heated by a fire underneath it, the copper provided all the hot water needed for the wash, which was also placed in it for the final boiling.

The most important laundering implement was a corrugated washboard of wood, glass or metal which stood in a tubful of hot, soapy water; some models actually incorporated the board into the tub, which was sold as a unit. Rubbing the cloth fairly gently against the board was effective in most cases, but heavily soiled linen required more vigorous treatment. So did materials that had been left unwashed for long periods, a practice that was quite common until late in the 19th century. Infrequent wash-days minimized the disruption of the household and also became a matter of social prestige, as they demonstrated that the family in question had a more than ample supply of clothing and domestic linen.

## THE WASHING DOLLY

The housewife or laundress used a variety of simple aids to agitate the wash. The washing dolly, or dolly peg, was a long wooden stick with a crossbar near the top; the base resembled a stool, with several stumps splaying out from a small horizontal disc. The dolly was thrust deep into the tub and moved up and down and round and round – a mode of agitation that was effective enough to be imitated in the earliest practical washing machines. A similar device was the punch, a long stick which ended in a cylinder with notches cut out from the sides. The posser consisted of a perforated cone, usually made of copper, attached to a long handle. It achieved its effect partly through suction.

For a heavy wash, the stout wooden-staved tubs which had been used for centuries were eventually replaced in towns by barrel-shaped metal 'dolly tubs' with corrugated sides (with or without built-in washboards). These were still being advertised and sold in Britain in the 1930s and 1940s, after which time the majority of people were able to afford electric washing machines.

After soaking and washing – and intermittent wringing and rinsing – the wash was boiled in the copper, where it was moved about and ultimately lifted out with a stick. With their love of gadgetry, the Victorians came up with at least one ingenious variation on this simple functional object – the Eastlake Clothes Stick, comprising two linked hollow tubes designed to allow water to run off from the linen – and probably all over the laundress!

### DRYING AND AIRING

When the washing (including blueing, starching and other processes) was finally done, it had to be dried. In the country, the linen could be laid out on the grass or hedges, or pegged on to a line. The simplest kind of peg – a slit piece of wood strengthened with a steel band – seems to have been mainly made and sold by

◀ *For poorer families living in rural areas, washday could involve all the female members of the household, including quite young children. Daughters might peg the clothes or be sent off to gather up linen drying in the fields, or asked to collect washing from neighbours if their mother took in laundry.*

▲ *These essential pieces of equipment for the Edwardian laundress are, from left to right: a galvanized steel scrubbing bath containing a washing bat, two scrubbing boards, a two-handled wooden carrier for washing, some wooden pegs and a galvanized steel bucket for carrying water.*

sometimes put on china 'feet', for example.

Last of all came smoothing, with or without an iron. Sheets and table linen in large households were usually smoothed with a linen press, consisting of a frame within which a heavy board could be lowered by turning a handle. The press was placed on top of a chest or cupboard in which the finished linen could be stored; inevitably, from the late 19th century, some presses were manufactured with their own built-in drawers.

gypsies; this has become a collectable in its own right, like its successors, the hand-turned dolly peg and the spring-clip peg. Lines were also used in towns, although smuts and specks from the polluted atmosphere often spoiled the laundress's handiwork. The alternative was to dry the washing indoors, despite the inconvenience involved, and an extensive range of clothes-horses with racks or radiating spokes was developed; it included ingenious devices that could be raised to the ceiling in order to save space. Clothes could also be kept in shape by being dried over objects with appropriate contours – socks were

# The Modern Kitchen

The kitchen of the inter-war years was compact,
practical and light – altogether a pleasant room where
the family could eat together

In the grander houses built during the Victorian era, the kitchen was invariably relegated to the basement, and the division between the servants who worked in the dark and uncomfortable rooms 'below stairs' and the polite society above, was absolute. By the 1920s, however, smaller homes, the decline of domestic service and the advances of technology made a different kind of kitchen both necessary and possible. Clumsy ranges, dark passages, awkward stairs and anterooms – larders, butteries and pantries – were on the way out to be replaced by built-in cupboards, streamlined units and new labour-saving devices. At the same time, materials such as chrome, stainless steel and enamel were taking over from iron, copper and deal. The kitchen moved out of the gloom of the basement and into the light of the ground floor, and a new awareness of kitchen planning made for a more rational arrangement of furniture in which everything was conveniently close at hand.

*Bright colours, easy-to-clean surfaces and a new cosiness and compactness marked the advent of the modern kitchen – a far cry from the dark Victorian days.*

furniture store, was usually simple and functional. The legs were straight and undecorated while the top could be enamel or stainless steel, or covered with lino. The chairs were simple too; they were usually made of beech or birch, and often rush-seated. Meals were prepared on the kitchen table, and on informal family occasions, eaten there too.

Cookers were either electric or gas although gas cookers were actually more popular because electricity was the more expensive fuel. Furthermore, the advent of the Regulo thermostat in 1923, which meant that the oven could be self-regulating, reinforced the preference for gas. Cookers came in pressed steel, with easy-to-clean enamel. They were available in a range of colours, but the most common were mottled green or grey, with a white enamelled

In the 1920s and 1930s a great deal of thought was devoted to the arrangement of the three principal elements of the kitchen: the sink, the table and the cooker. An American time and motion expert at the time calculated that a cook took an average of 281 steps while making a cake in an unplanned kitchen. The same process involved only 45 steps in a correctly planned room.

The sink, previously made of iron or stone, was now enamel or stainless steel, both of which were much easier to clean. For example, in the *Staybrite Book* of 1934, produced to bring Firth and Brown of Sheffield's stainless steel to a wider public, a model kitchen was shown with stainless-steel draining board and sink accompanied by numerous stainless-steel items including cutlery and mixing bowl.

### HOT RUNNING WATER

A gas water heater could be positioned above the sink to provide hot running water if there was not an independent domestic boiler, such as the popular 'Ideal'. The sink was located near the window, so that the mother could keep an eye on the children playing in the garden.

The kitchen table, purchased from the local

▲ *A suburban housewife washes up in a typical inter-war kitchen. The half-tiling with green border tiles surmounted by cream walls, grey gas cooker and built-in recess for pots and pans are all characteristic features.*

▲▶ *The first electric kettles appeared around 1900. This example from the 1930s resembles the copper kettles found on Victorian kitchen ranges.*

▶ *Not all women were full-time housewives, but they were expected to maintain high standards of domestic efficiency. Numerous women's magazines appeared giving useful hints for the servantless household.*

*◄ A modern room with an eclectic style that recreates the homely feel of a 1930s kitchen. Jacobethan chairs and table are placed in the centre of the room. A built in pine dresser on the left houses an assortment of pottery and crocks, while a chimney recess contains an old-fashioned cooker. 1930s china, a mantelpiece clock and toby jugs all add further period touches.*

half-tiled, with a patterned tile border at the top.

For the floor, cork tiles were an attractive new innovation, and plywood was sometimes used as parquet. Magnesite (a kind of plastic), rubber and cellulose floors were also available. Lino was popular and came in a range of colours and patterns. One of its attractions was that it could be easily mopped clean, not like the old stone flat floors which, cold, hard and unyielding, had to be scrubbed.

The traditional dresser, though difficult to dust, was not immediately abandoned in favour of fitted cupboards. It evolved into the kitchen cabinet, a piece of furniture that was for practical use as well as – or instead of – display. It had cupboards, drawers and shelves, for crockery, cutlery and pans. It also boasted useful fitments such as glass storage jars and

door which gave a clean, practical finish. Early oven doors had an iron latch, which later gave way to a Bakelite handle.

### STREAMLINED CUPBOARDS

Lining the walls of the kitchen were a range of cupboards – tall ones used as larders or to house brooms, and smaller ones for general storage. Some of the cupboards carried a fold-out or slide-out enamel-topped work surface. The walls were painted white, or a pale colour. They were often

*◄ A sturdy-looking cast-iron Salter kitchen scale with an enamel face. In an age which valued speed and convenience, these spring action scales came to replace the out-dated Victorian versions with their balances and weights: the busy housewife found them far quicker and easier to use.*

---

# *The Pressure Cooker*

STEAMING HAD LONG BEEN USED AS A COOKING METHOD, BUT THE ADVENT OF THE PRESSURE COOKER ADDED A NEW DIMENSION TO THE TECHNIQUE BY COMBINING STEAM WITH PRESSURE TO COOK FOODS IN A FRACTION OF THE TIME THEY NORMALLY TOOK. PRESSURE COOKERS FIRST BECAME WIDELY AVAILABLE IN THE 1930s. THEY WERE MARKETED AS 'HEALTH COOKERS', AND SAID TO BE THE SCIENTIFIC SOLUTION TO ALL DIETRY DEFICIENCIES AND MOST OF THE ILLS OF MODERN CIVILISATION, BECAUSE THEY SEALED IN THE PRECIOUS NUTRIENTS THAT WERE LOST IN CONVENTIONAL COOKING METHODS. ALL THIS APPEALED GREATLY TO THE THEN FASHIONABLE OBSESSION WITH HEALTH AND EFFICIENCY. IT WAS FURTHER CLAIMED THAT THE FLAVOURS AND TENDERNESS OF MEATS, VEGETABLES AND PUDDINGS WERE ENHANCED BY PRESSURE COOKING, MAKING THE PROCESS GASTRONOMICALLY ATTRACTIVE. BESIDES THESE NUTRITIONAL ADVANTAGES, PUBLICITY BROCHURES WAXED LYRICAL ABOUT THE AMOUNT OF TIME AND LABOUR SAVED BY THE NEW METHOD. ONCE THE COOKER HAD BEEN PUT ON THE STOVE AND THE DIAL SET, THE HOUSEWIFE COULD ATTEND TO OTHER DUTIES UNTIL THE WHISTLE BLEW, SIGNALLING THAT THE MEAL WAS READY.

*◄ A 1930s EASIWORK HEALTH COOKER. SPECIAL RACKS INSIDE MEANT THAT AN ENTIRE MEAL COULD BE COOKED AT ONCE, WITH MEAT AND POTATOES PLACED ON THE BOTTOM, VEGETABLES IN THE MIDDLE, AND STEWED FRUIT OR PEAS AND BEANS AT THE TOP.*

▶ *A metal and Bakelite toaster dating from the 1930s. The inter-war years saw a steady rise in the number of homes connected to the mains electricity supply, and consequently an enormous increase in the number of electrical appliances in the kitchen.*

◀ *A sketch from 1936 illustrating an ideal kitchen layout. Cream coloured walls and kitchen units, combined with streamlined design create an impression of light and space, and much use is made of new materials like tubular steel and Vitrolite. Pride of place is given to the Aga cooker – an updated version of the traditional range.*

little glass drawers, a flour dispenser, and a pastry board which dropped down or slid out.

In the inter-war years, the housewife had to do most of her own housework for the first time. She was expected to keep house to a very high standard, and housework began to be viewed as a 'career' with popular magazines heralding the housewife as the operator of the 'domestic workshop' of the kitchen. She wanted some time to herself as well, of course, and this was made possible by labour-saving gadgets such as Hoovers and polishers, which were often given away to new house purchasers as a sales ploy. The spread of electricity was the prime factor in

the advent of labour-saving items: in 1910 only 2 per cent of people in Britain had electricity, but by 1939 the figure was 75 per cent.

The first efficient electric kettle, in which the element was actually immersed in the water rather than placed beneath it, was the 'Swan', introduced by Bulpitt and Son of Birmingham in the early 1920s. Amongst the range of other convenient appliances

▼ *In this 1931 advertisment a party of elegantly dressed men and women gather round to admire the latest acquisition – a refrigerator. At this date a fridge was still a luxury, but by the end of the decade most homes had one.*

▼ *Electric food mixers appeared in the 1930s. These labour-saving gadgets were a blessing for the modern cook with little time or domestic help.*

were pressure cookers, food mixers and electric hot plates. Plastic was starting to become important too – although it was not the inexpensive alternative it is now. Plastic tableware was widely available, but there were also plastic wall laminates and plastic draining boards, which were bright and very practical, and even a pyramid-shaped Bakelite toaster.

### ELECTRICAL APPLIANCES

Early refrigerators were expensive. In the 1920s frigidaires cost around £60 – about as much as a new car. The Electrolux models of the late 1920s had a cork-lined wooden cabinet, and had to be connected to constant running water. As the technology improved, running water was no longer necessary, the fridge became cheaper, and it took on the classic form of white-enamelled steel that we know today. By the late 1930s, fridges were quite

common electrical appliances often bought on hire-purchase.

The washing machine had not yet evolved into its modern form. Many people had a wash-boiler; an enamelled tub on legs in which water was heated by gas or electricity and the clothes agitated with a wooden dolly. It was not long, however, before the dolly developed into electrically-powered paddles, and the machine took on its modern appearance.

### MODERN LIVING

The changes that took place in the kitchen were reflected in family life as a whole. Meals, whether taken in the dining room or the kitchen, were a time for the whole family to come together and dining room and kitchen were often separated only by a hatch. Gone were the severe, formal procedures of the Victorian dining room and the primitive and remote kitchens of the past.

## ◄ LIFE AND LEISURE ►
# *The Modern Cooker*

THE DUST AND SMOKE CREATED BY THE COAL RANGE WAS NOT ACCEPTABLE TO THE MODERN HOUSEWIFE, WHO PREFERRED THE CLEANLINESS AND EFFICIENCY OF GAS AND ELECTRIC COOKERS. ALTHOUGH GAS COOKERS HAD FIRST APPEARED IN VICTORIAN TIMES, THEY WERE REGARDED WITH A CERTAIN AMOUNT OF SUSPICION, AND IT WAS FEARED THAT SERVANTS WOULD NOT UNDERSTAND HOW THEY WORKED. BECAUSE OF THIS, THEY DID NOT BECOME REALLY POPULAR UNTIL AFTER WORLD WAR I. SALES OF ELECTRIC COOKERS WERE SLOWER TO TAKE OFF; THEY WERE MORE EXPENSIVE THAN GAS COOKERS, AND IT WAS NOT UNTIL THE END OF THE 1930S THAT MOST HOMES HAD ELECTRICITY. BUT THE DEVELOPMENT OF RELIABLE THERMOSTATS, AND THE AVAILABILITY OF HIRE PURCHASE FACILITIES, DID MUCH TO BOOST DEMAND IN THE PRE-WAR YEARS.

▲ THIS PUBLICITY POSTER MADE TO PROMOTE THE SALE OF ELECTRIC COOKERS EMPHASIZES THE COOLNESS AND HYGIENE OF THE PRODUCT, AND THE FACT THAT IT DOES NOT CREATE CLOUDS OF SMOKE.

▶ THIS POSTER CLEVERLY UNDERLINES ONE OF THE MAIN ADVANTAGES OF THE GAS COOKER — THE FACT THAT IT HEATS UP MORE QUICKLY THAN AN ELECTRIC ONE, ENABLING THE HOUSEWIFE TO SERVE MEALS ON TIME.

# Kitchen Furniture

## The new, smaller kitchens, designed for the smaller families of the 1920s and 1930s, required space-saving furniture that was easy to clean

The kitchen of the 1930s was the product of a social revolution. While the men were away from home during World War I, millions of women worked in offices and factories. New experiences and opportunities made them more independent-minded, and after the war it became apparent that few of them would go back into service – and that many wives would no longer put up with needless drudgery. This was particularly true of the middle-class woman, who had formerly concerned herself only with the selection of a menu and was now cast as chief cook and child-minder. She assumed her role willingly enough, but insisted on being supplied with adequate equipment and pleasant surroundings.

### An Integral Kitchen

If servants were fewer in the 1920s and 1930s, families were also smaller, and newly built houses reflected these trends in their compactness. As a result, the kitchen was integrated into the home: instead of being one or two floors away from the main living area, it lay just on the other side of a door or serving hatch. So everybody – husbands included – now had frequent contact with the kitchen and thus wanted it to be a clean, cheerful, attractive place.

Situated on the ground floor, it was smaller, brighter and neater than its Victorian and Edwardian predecessors, decorated in lighter colours and provided with a larger window area – which, among other things, enabled the housewife to keep an eye on her children when they played out in the garden.

### Fitted Cupboards

Cleanliness and convenience were at a premium. Tiles and other wipe-clean substances such as Vitrolite protected large areas of wall. Floors were covered with linoleum. At least two tall built-in cupboards became common – the broom cupboard, and the pantry or larder with tiled shelves, gauze window and possibly an electric fan to keep perishables cool. The main work surface, the table in the centre of the room, usually had a metal or linoleum top. And tubular steel kitchen furniture – at once modern in appearance and easy to wipe down – became quite popular, despite the condescending attitude of one authority, who held that 'chromed-steel bar stools evoke an amateurish levity hardly consonant with the serious business of cooking'!

In the new atmosphere of the 1920s,

▶ *This advertisement from 1936 exemplifies modern kitchen design. The stainless steel sink unit looks forward to today's fitted kitchens. Beige and red was one of the era's standard colour schemes.*

◀ *Just thirty years separate this 'modern style' Edwardian dresser from kitchen cabinets. Solid and imposing, the dresser was built for display in a large kitchen rather than for unobtrusive storage.*

many earlier innovations such as gas and electric cookers and vacuum cleaners were streamlined, mass-produced and brought into ordinary homes for the first time. After almost 150 years the kitchen range became obsolete, its functions taken over by the 'Ideal' boiler which produced hot water, and by cookers with their distinctive blue, grey or green speckled enamel cases and white oven doors.

### Luxury Appliances

Although manufactured, washing machines and refrigerators remained luxury items, found in few British homes until after World War II; however, the pantry, and objects such as frost boxes and meat safes, helped to extend the life-span of perishables. The British housewife was already intensely gadget-conscious, and catalogues were full of devices for chopping, mincing, slicing, straining, steaming and toasting, as well as electric kettles, coffee-makers and even such

*◀ Simple, functional 1930s furniture goes well in today's kitchens. Some tasteful repainting helps; too much lessens value.*

*▲ Combining storage space with an enamelled worktop, cabinets like this were a space-saving boon in the compact 1930s kitchens.*

marvels as a 'Magic Marmalade Machine'.

Another striking new feature was the free-standing kitchen cabinet which replaced the decorative but over-large and dust-attracting dresser. In Britain the pioneer was a furniture manufacturer named Len Cooklin, who began producing kitchen cabinets with a staff of five in a room above a Liverpool garage. The earliest cabinets were of exceptional quality, made of oak or ash and individually signed by the craftsman responsible. Cooklin's venture prospered, and in 1925 it was incorporated – and became a household name – as Hygena Ltd. By this time Heal's and other manufacturers had entered the market, producing cabinets to suit all purses and vying with one another in devising ways of economizing space and including labour-saving devices. An efficiently ventilated, multi-compartmented object that functioned as both store cupboard and work surface, the kitchen cabinet became a familiar sight in every well-equipped home between the wars.

By the 1930s some designers were already anticipating the present-day built-in, continuous-surface kitchen. But for the overwhelming majority of people between the wars, the small, bright, centre-table kitchen, with its cabinet and cooker, represented all that was desirable, liberating and modern.

# The 1930s Kitchen Cabinet

KITCHEN CABINETS HAD THEIR HEYDAY IN THE INTER-WAR YEARS, FORMING A BRIDGE BETWEEN THE VICTORIAN OR EDWARDIAN DRESSER AND THE MODERN FITTED KITCHEN, AND THEIR DESIGN ILLUSTRATES SEVERAL 1930S THEMES.

FROSTED OR STAINED GLASS DOORS WERE TYPICAL, AND THE SUNBURST WAS A POPULAR DESIGN. SOME HAD NATURAL WOOD FINISHES, BUT THEY WERE MORE COMMONLY PAINTED. THE CASE WAS ALWAYS PAINTED A DIFFERENT COLOUR FROM THE DOORS AND DRAWER-FRONTS, WHILE THE PLASTIC HANDLES MATCHED THE MAIN CABINET COLOUR. STANDARD COLOUR SCHEMES FEATURED A STRONG BLUE, GREEN OR RED CONTRASTING WITH CREAM, OFF-WHITE OR BEIGE.

SOME CABINETS HAD A CENTRAL DOOR THAT DROPPED DOWN TO FORM A WORK TOP. OTHERS, LIKE THIS ONE, HAD A MORE STABLE PULL-OUT ENAMELLED WORKING SURFACE.

① STAINED-GLASS SUNBURST PATTERN ON DOORS

② PULL-OUT ENAMELLED WORK SURFACE

③ DOORS PAINTED IN CONTRASTING COLOUR TO CASE

④ PLASTIC HANDLES MATCHING COLOUR OF CASE

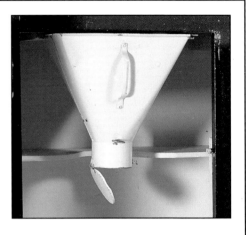

INTEGRAL FLOUR DISPENSERS HARKED BACK TO THE DAYS WHEN MOST HOUSEHOLDS STILL BAKED THEIR OWN BREAD.

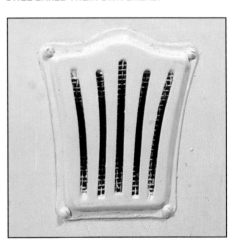

SOME DOORS HAD VENTILATION GRILLES SO THAT THE CUPBOARDS COULD BE USED TO STORE PERISHABLE FOODS.

## Utility Cabinet

DURING THE WAR, CERTAIN FURNISHING MATERIALS BECAME SCARCE AND CRAFTSMEN WERE DIVERTED INTO THE WAR EFFORT. AS SUPPLIES OF FURNITURE DRIED UP, SO DEMAND GREW, PARTICULARLY FROM THOSE WHO HAD BEEN BOMBED OUT. IN 1943 THE GOVERNMENT INTRODUCED THE UTILITY RANGE TO MEET THE GROWING NEED. THERE WERE 20 BASIC DESIGNS INCLUDING THE CABINET ILLUSTRATED HERE. QUALITY AND PRICE WERE BOTH CONTROLLED, AND THE RANGE WAS BUILT TO LAST. DESIGN RESTRICTIONS WERE LIFTED IN 1948 AND THE RANGE WAS DISCONTINUED IN 1952.

The 1930s kitchen cabinet was a cleverly designed multi-purpose object that combined a discreet appearance with a fascinating space-efficiency.

The kitchen cabinet was free-standing, so it could be placed anywhere in the kitchen, according to convenience. Most versions shared the same basic structure of a base unit comprising two cupboards with drawers above (similar to today's sink units) topped with a double cupboard of shallower depth.

Inside, an elaborate, well-thought-out arrangement of compartments, shelves and hooks made it possible for the housewife to store cutlery, food, condiments and cleaning materials, with each item in its allotted place. The cabinet even held perishables, since the compartments were provided with ventilation grilles; and the most sophisticated models included an extraordinary range of extras — utensils, storage-jars, a flour dispenser, egg and spice racks, and even a shopping check list. What made the kitchen cabinet the last word in functionalism was its handy pull-down or pull-out work surface, which tucked neatly away when not in use. Pull-down work surfaces provided temporary storage space for items needed for chores on

## Kitchen Furniture

▲ A BROOM CUPBOARD CABINET IN ENAMELLED ALUMINIUM.

PRICE GUIDE **4**

▲ THIS KITCHEN CABINET, STILL IN ITS ORIGINAL LIVERY, HAS DECORATED GLASS DOORS.

PRICE GUIDE **5**

▲ THIS CABINET HAS A NATURAL WOOD FINISH MADE FROM STAINED PINE AND PLYWOOD.

PRICE GUIDE **4**

▲ SCHOLL PRODUCED THIS TUBULAR STEEL CHAIR WITH AN ADJUSTABLE BACK.

PRICE GUIDE **4**

▲ LIGHT AND EASY TO CLEAN, TUBULAR STEEL WAS IDEAL FOR 1930S KITCHEN FURNITURE.

PRICE GUIDE **4**

▲ A BEECHWOOD KITCHEN TABLE FROM THE 1930S WITH A TYPICAL ENAMEL TOP.

PRICE GUIDE **4**

▲ BENT, STAINED BEECHWOOD AND PLYWOOD FOLDING CHAIR.

PRICE GUIDE **3**

the kitchen table, but tended to be flimsy, and so were not ideal for heavier tasks or weights. The pull-out variety were more practical and usually featured a wipe-clean covering of enamel or aluminium.

Although some 1930s kitchen cabinets were rather utilitarian in appearance many display the type of decoration and use of colour that have come to be characteristic of the period.

Cupboard doors were made more interesting by the use of inset panels of glass or mesh.

Frosted glass was popular, as were designs in imitation of stained glass windows and leaded lights.

The more solid cabinets were made in dark stained oak or pine while cheaper plywood carcasses were disguised with a paint finish, pastel colours such as green, cream and pale blue being typical. Some cupboards were even made entirely of lightweight aluminium although these were more usually part of the type of kitchen furniture suites that proved to be the

predecessors of the modern fitted kitchen.

All in all, the cabinet constituted a mini-kitchen, useful to the suburban housewife and ideal in poor people's cramped quarters or in the recessed kitchens or kitchenettes being installed in some advanced apartment designs.

Today the 1930s kitchen cupboard is more often seen doubling as a storage unit in the garden shed than in shops specialising in Art Deco furniture, and the speculative collector

may still find bargains in local junk shops or tucked away, unregarded in second-hand furniture stores.

### POINTS TO WATCH
■ Make sure that inset glass and mesh panels and cupboard handles are original.
■ Cabinets with interesting interior features such as flour dispensers are more collectable.
■ Chipped paint finishes can be re-touched but a complete overhaul will limit a cabinet's collectability.

# Plastic Tableware

Essential for the fashionable 1930s kitchen, ranges of the new plastic tableware were renowned for their modern designs and bold colours.

Plastic consumer goods reached the mass-market for the first time during the inter-war period. Their introduction was triggered mainly by the world shortage of natural materials such as rubber, ivory and silk. By the 1930s an enormous variety of plastic goods was available, including tableware, which soon proved to be an acceptable alternative to ceramics.

Today, early plastic antiques, or 'plastiques', are collectors' items and are valued as much for what they reveal about the history of the plastics industry as for their Deco designs. While many plastics are now out of the reach of the average collector, tableware can be more accessible, particularly the smaller mouldings such as napkin rings, ashtrays or picnicware.

### NATURAL PLASTICS

Any material which is capable of being moulded by heat or pressure can be termed 'plastic', and natural plastics like horn have been ground and compressed into snuff boxes and decorative trinkets since the 18th century. The modern plastics industry evolved from 19th-century experiments to find cheap substitutes for rare and expensive natural materials like tortoiseshell, amber, lacquer and horn. Plastics were soon found to be particularly suited to mass-production techniques employed to satisfy the ever-growing population.

Alexander Parkes, a Birmingham inventor, is generally credited as being the father of the industry, and the inventor of the first semi-synthetic plastic to find a large, domestic market. Parkesine, his mouldable cellulose nitrate dough, was exhibited at the Universal Exhibition of 1862. It could be manufactured in a range of multichrome or plain colours, and was pressed into decorative plaques, hair slides, combs and knife handles.

Unfortunately, its behaviour proved rather unpredictable. Plastic combs were returned after a couple of months' wear so warped and misshapen that they were unusable. Other Parkesine mouldings became brittle and cracked and after only a few years' trading, Parkes's company was forced into liquidation. These early pieces, made between 1862 and 1868, are consequently extremely rare and are really museum rather than collectors' items.

Parkes's associate, Daniel Spill, continued to manufacture similar plastics which simulated wood and ivory, and which were marketed as Xylonite and Ivoride. Spill had no more commercial success than Parkes and his company, and the British Xylonite Company teetered on the brink of collapse until it captured the enormous market for stiff, washable collars made of celluloid, which became popular at the turn of the century.

### THE INTRODUCTION OF CELLULOID

Celluloid was originally patented in America by Isaiah and John Wesley Hyatt, who discovered a method of plasticising cellulose nitrate with camphor in a way which left the plastic far less brittle. By the 1870s, when ivory was in short supply, celluloid was widely used to manufacture billiard balls, knife handles, napkin rings, dolls, dressing table sets and thousands of other decorative items in 'ivory', 'tortoiseshell' or 'pearl' finishes. Celluloid's commercial reputation suffered, however, as a result of fires in the new 'moving picture' houses which started

## Beetleware Plastic

THIS UNUSUAL BEAKER, MOULDED IN SCARAB AND BEETLE PLASTICS, WAS MANUFACTURED BY THE BEETLE PRODUCTS COMPANY WHICH BECAME SO WELL KNOWN IN THE 1930S.

*Until recent years the only plastics considered worthy of appearing at auction were clocks or furniture inlaid with casein. Today it is a fast growing field for the collector. The major advantage of collecting plastics is their widespread availability; they can be found almost anywhere including local jumble sales. Perhaps surprisingly, many people now collect Deco tableware for its visual appeal and striking designs.*

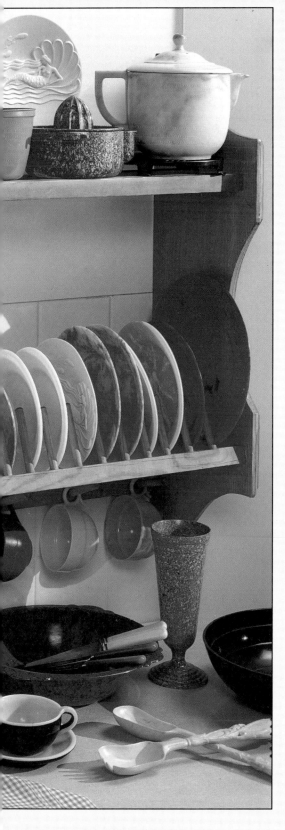

*Taken from the Bandalasta catalogue of 1928, this shows the extensive range of plastic tableware available at the time. The company's main selling point was the durability and cheapness of their products. They made no attempt to imitate more traditional tableware designs or materials and relied on the attractiveness of their mottled designs for visual appeal.*

when the highly flammable celluloid film caught alight.

Another early semi-synthetic plastic was Casein, discovered by the Bavarian chemist, Adolf Spitteler. His cat apparently knocked a bottle of formaldehyde solution over a saucer of milk, leading to the invention of a plastic widely admired for its lustrous, milky quality which was used to simulate amber, ivory, pearl, tortoiseshell, agate and malachite. It was marketed in England from 1914 under the trade name Erinoid and proved extremely popular for cutlery handles, napkin rings and dressing-table sets. Its tendency to retain moisture, however, made it an impractical material for most tableware items.

### BAKELITE

The first real breakthrough in moulding a plastic with good insulating and water-resisting properties came with Bakelite, a phenol formaldehyde resin patented by Leo Baekeland in 1909. Bakelite was the first totally man-made, synthetic plastic. The trade name 'Bakelite' is now loosely used to describe all phenolic plastics which share its distinctive dark mottled brown, red or green appearance.

Bakelite proved suitable for a vast range of consumer goods. Its heat resistance made it the ideal material for electrical products like hairdryers and radios, for smoking accessories and for kitchen equipment and utensil handles. A few beakers were made in Bakelite, but in contact with hot liquids, the plastic gave off an unpleasant smell and flavoured the drink. Another serious drawback was the fact that Bakelite could only be made in dark colours, because of the fillers needed to strengthen the resin.

It was Beetle thiorea formaldehyde which brought a totally new look to picnic and tableware in the late 1920s, and finally satisfied the need for a clean-smelling, hygienic-looking, light-coloured plastic suitable for storing and serving food.

### BANDALASTA TABLEWARE

In 1926 a Harrods window display of bright and attractively mottled Linga Longa and Bandalasta wares caused a sensation. They were moulded using the new, white powders marketed by the Beetle Products Company. In the early 1930s, a paper-filled urea formaldehyde superseded the thiorea, and soon moulding companies all over Britain were able to create an expansive range of tableware, from condiment sets and cutlery to candlesticks and cocktail shakers.

Beetle plastics soon graced every fashionable kitchen, complementing the new plastic draining boards, toasters, utensils, plate racks, knobs, switches and handles and the new-look 'easicleen' laminated surfaces. The modern housewife could at last surround herself with the plastic props which were recommended in magazines as offering cleanliness, convenience, and 'a toughness and modernness that has a definite and good psychological effect'.

# Tableware

**D**ark, phenolic plastics were often used to make eggcups, napkin rings, ashtrays, candlesticks, bowls and biscuit containers.

The pale-coloured urea formaldehyde was far more extensively used for tableware – and particularly for items that came into contact with food and hot liquids. Bandalasta was one of the earliest and most expensive lines, moulded by Brookes & Adams from 1927-32.

The typical marbled colours of Bandalasta were achieved by sprinkling or mixing powders ground to different consistencies. The powders were packed into steel moulds and shaped under pressure and heat, which made the plastic flow.

The largest manufacturer of plastic tableware in England was the Streetly Manufacturing Company, whose Beetleware – much of it moulded for Woolworth's – became a best-selling plastic line, rather more affordable than Bandalasta.

Profiles too became more streamlined as plastic design broke away from its earlier imitation of traditional ceramic shapes, following a style of its own.

▶ *Green and cream marbled teapot in Bandalasta Ware made from coloured moulding powders.*

PRICE GUIDE **3**

▲ *These 1930s beakers are made in thio urea formaldehyde, coloured in imitation of horn.*

PRICE GUIDE **3**

▼ *An orange squeezer and toast rack made in urea formaldehyde.*

PRICE GUIDE **3**

**PRICE GUIDE**

▼ *Part of a breakfast set of the popular Beetleware comprising plates, bowls and milk jug.*

PRICE GUIDE **4**

▲ *This fruitbowl is made from Thetford Pulpware, a wood pulp covered in green and gilt plastic.*

PRICE GUIDE **1**

◀ *A mottled black and white salt pot made in the 1930s from urea formaldehyde.*

PRICE GUIDE **1**

▼ *Marbled orange jampot made in thio urea formaldehyde by Beetleware.*

PRICE GUIDE **2**

◀ *A breakfast set in marbled orange and cream Bandalasta with a cream perspex toast rack, set on a mottled brown tray.*

PRICE GUIDE **5**

◀ *From matching set of egg-cups and cups and saucers, in mottled brown thio urea formaldehyde*

PRICE GUIDE **4**

PRICE GUIDE

# Picnic Hampers

By the 1920s, the sort of picnic envisaged by Mrs. Beeton, with at least 120 bottles of liquor for 40 participants, was nothing but a memory – along with the regiment of servants required to orchestrate such a grand event.

Eating alfresco, however, was still popular, and it was at the motoring, boating, and camping parties of the 1920s and 1930s that plastic products scored their greatest triumph. In fact, picnickers were specifically targeted in the plastic manufacturer's advertising campaigns.

Picnic boxes and hampers became 'miracles of compactness and utility', with closely-packed nests of beakers, plates, and food containers which were more durable than china and half the weight.

The picnic box itself was frequently manufactured in woven cellulose acetate, or coated with a plastic imitation leather, and occasionally stood on handy, folding legs. Com-

panies like Glenco, Coracle, Brexton and the well-known luggage specialists, Revelation, would design the box or basket and buy in a complementary line of plastic picnicware.

The designs for tableware and picnicware were interchangeable, although a special

picnic cup was made with a circular handle to allow for stacking. Butter and sugar pots with plastic lids fitted neatly inside the cups.

The Bandalasta 'tennis set' was also purpose-made, with a teacup which sat firmly on a palette-shaped plate. To complete the set, a thermos flask moulded in urea formaldehyde in a complementary colour was available from Thermos Ltd.

◀ Made by Coracle for Harrods in the 1930s, this wicker picnic basket has a comprehensive range of Bandalasta ware and even a plastic ground-sheet.

PRICE GUIDE **6**

PRICE GUIDE

▶ *Neatly packed in a snakeskin case, this marbled green plastic picnic set is made in urea formaldehyde and comprises cups, plates and food containers.*

PRICE GUIDE 4

◀ *Making full use of the virtues of the new plastics, this flask by Thermos Ltd., has a simple, streamlined shape and is both lightweight and hygienic.*

PRICE GUIDE 2

▼ *An early version of Tupperware, 1930s Bandalasta was ideal for picnics.*

PRICE GUIDE 1

◀ *Thermos flask made in Roanoid, a form of urea formaldehyde.*

PRICE GUIDE 2

◀ *By Thermos Ltd., this flask is made in phenolic formaldehyde.*

PRICE GUIDE 2

PRICE GUIDE

## COLLECTOR'S TIPS

Street markets are usually the best place to search for 'plastiques'. Plenty of small mouldings like eggcups, napkin rings and beakers or other pieces of picnicware survive. Chrome and plastic cocktail shakers and thermos flasks are also quite common, although the larger and more decorative items of tableware – cakestands, candlesticks, tablelamps and fruit bowls – are becoming increasingly difficult to find.

### UTILITARIAN BUT BRITTLE

This is partly because interest in collecting plastics has escalated in the last few years, and decorative tableware is prized above the more utilitarian pieces. It is also because the urea formaldehyde plastics readily chipped and cracked when dropped, or developed hairline cracks and stains and partially disintegrated after heavy use or prolonged contact with hot liquids. Much plastic tableware, therefore, has long since been consigned to the dustbin, and it was never manufactured on a scale to rival the most popular ceramic lines by Clarice Cliff or Susie Cooper.

Collectors of picnicware would be extremely lucky to find a complete set, with its original basket or box, and a Bandalasta set in mint condition might fetch hundreds of pounds. With patience, however, it should be possible to fill gaps in a collection by buying individual pieces from different markets.

Bandalasta ware, undoubtedly the Rolls Royce of the plastic tableware industry, is the most sought-after trade name today. Made of urea thiorea formaldehyde, it has a certain solidity and a substantial feel which some of the later paper-filled urea formaldehyde plastics lack.

### CRAFTSMANSHIP AND FINISH

Brookes & Adams, who manufactured Bandalasta, also used extremely good quality steel dies and the pieces were given a high degree of finish. 'Flashings' – or the thin lines of plastic which seep out at the joints between two halves of a mould – were tooled away, and this marks the difference between a good and a poor quality moulding. Bases on Bandalasta bowls were also secured with brass rather than base metal screws.

The beautiful, marbled colourings were not quite matched by any other company, and because of the method of manufacture – with powders mixed in varying proportions and sprinkled into the moulds – no two pieces are exactly alike.

Bandalasta ware is often twice as expensive as other makes: an ordinary Beetle teapot might fetch over twice as much with the Bandalasta trademark on the base. You should also expect to pay high prices for the large, decorative fruit and rose bowls. Colour also affects the price: ivory marbled with orange, for example, is much less sought-after than Bandarouge, a rich mix-

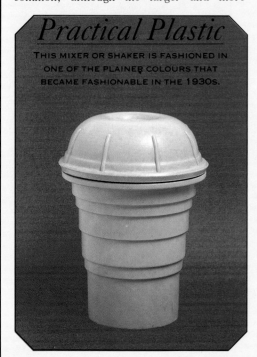

### Practical Plastic

THIS MIXER OR SHAKER IS FASHIONED IN ONE OF THE PLAINER COLOURS THAT BECAME FASHIONABLE IN THE 1930S.

# Jaxonite Biscuit Barrel

ALTHOUGH MOST PLASTIC TABLEWARE WAS SPECIFICALLY DESIGNED TO BE PRACTICAL AND DURABLE, ONE PARTICULAR RANGE WAS PRODUCED WITH A MORE DECORATIVE PURPOSE IN MIND. THIS WAS KNOWN AS JAXONITE, WHICH COMBINED A DARK MOTTLED BODY OF UREA FORMALDEHYDE, AS USED FOR BANDALASTA WARE, WITH BEAUTIFULLY CRAFTED SILVER-PLATED FITTINGS. THE EFFECT THIS PRODUCED IS TYPICAL OF THE ART DECO FASHION FOR USING CONTRASTING COLOURS AND TEXTURES TO CREATE A DRAMATIC VISUAL EFFECT. LARGE JAXONITE BOWLS OR BISCUIT BARRELS WERE OFTEN BOUGHT AS WEDDING PRESENTS. THESE COULD BE MATCHED WITH A WHOLE RANGE OF TABLEWARE INCLUDING TABLE LAMPS, CANDLESTICKS AND COFFEE SETS.

① AFTER SETTING, MOULDINGS ARE TRIMMED AND POLISHED, USING SPECIAL MACHINERY

② MOTTLED PATTERNS ARE ACHIEVED BY THE BLENDING OF DIFFERENT COLOURED MOULDING POWDERS

③ SILVER-PLATED TRIMMINGS WERE USUALLY HALLMARKED

④ THE MARBLED EFFECT, POPULARIZED BY BANDALASTA IN 1928, WAS FASHIONABLE UNTIL THE MID-1930S

◆ *CLOSE UP* ◆

① BEETLEWARE

② BANDALASTA WARE

③ MOULDED PLASTIC

⑦ PARTING LINE

④ THETFORD PULPWARE

⑤ LINGA LONGA WARE

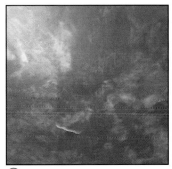

⑥ BANDALASTA PATTERNS

① BEETLEWARE MADE WITH BEATL UREA THIOUREA FORMALDEHYDE

② BANDALASTA, BY BROOKES & ADAMS FROM 1927-1932

③ THIS MOULDED PLATE IS MADE IN DARK-COLOURED BAKELITE

④ THETFORD PULPWARE IS MADE FROM WOOD PULP WHICH IS COATED IN SHINY PLASTIC

⑤ LINGA LONGA WARE MADE IN BEETLE PLASTIC

⑥ MOTTLED PATTERNS FROM BLENDED POWDER COLOURS

⑦ THE PARTING LINE IS KNOWN AS THE 'FLASH' AND IS OFTEN ONLY VISIBLE ON POORER QUALITY MOULDINGS

⑧ WELL MADE MOULDED PLASTIC ITEMS HAVE FINELY FORMED SHAPES WITH SMOOTH EDGES AND NO SEAMS.

⑧ MOULDED LINES

ture of red, orange, blue, green and yellow, and may cost only half as much.

Other trade names to look out for are Beaconware and Beetleware, both moulded by the Streetly Manufacturing Company, and Linga Longa. Names, pattern and patent numbers embossed on the base can reveal interesting information about the object, and it is generally wise to buy marked rather than unmarked pieces even though they are more expensive.

### IMITATIONS

Hundreds of companies plagiarized the shapes and colourings of the most popular lines; Belplastic, for example, made a cheaper version of the successful Bandalasta and Beetleware marbled picnic sets. Linsdenware, Stadium and Eloware all imitated Bakelite's woody, mottled appearance, but pieces carrying these names are all more valuable than anonymous copies.

There are plenty of themes for a collec-tion – buying according to material, manu-facturer or even moulding are all possibili-ties. Condiment sets, for example, were made in a huge range of shapes and colours, reflecting the changing tastes of the 1920s, 1930s and 1940s. It is possible to find salt cellars embossed with the stepped, odeones-que motif typical of the Art Deco period. Others moulded by Streetly for Woolworth's reflect an evolution from the hexagonal, faceted shape popular in the 1930s to the more streamlined, elongated egg-shape.

Collectors looking for very early, semi-synthetic plastics like Parkesine will most probably be disappointed; although an odd item occasionally comes up for sale at auction. Celluloid knife handles, napkin rings and salad servers can still be found, however, and it should be possible to buy decorative items made of casein.

The major problem facing new collectors is identification of the different materials. It can be extremely difficult to tell whether an object is genuine tortoiseshell, or an imita-tion in either celluloid or casein. Experts can distinguish the materials by flow marks or processing lines in the plastic, and by differences in feel, sound and smell. Cellu-loid smells faintly of camphor when rubbed, for example, and vulcanite (hard rubber) has a slightly sticky surface feel.

### EXPERT TESTS

More accurate analyses can be made with flame tests, using a tiny scraping of powder from a hidden part of the object. The smell and colour of the flame will identify the plastic. Casein, for example, smells of burning milk or cheese, while urea formal-dehyde smells fishy, like overheated elec-trics. These tests are best conducted by professionals. Most early plastics can be adequately cleaned with a damp cloth or soap and water, and rubbed with a non-abrasive metal polish to restore lustre. Harsh abrasives may scratch the surface.

# Recipe Books

**Pre-war cookery books, produced in attractive formats, fought hard, but largely in vain, to improve British cuisine**

While the vast majority of old books, including many acquired by collectors for their rarity, are doomed to gather dust unopened, you can be fairly certain that the owner of an old cookery book will consult it often, either in search of a recipe or simply for pleasure. It may be an acknowledged classic, which has had a profound influence on the development of British cooking, or it may have totally undistinguished recipes, which no one in their right mind would wish to recreate, but nevertheless be illustrated with charming wood-cuts or line drawings.

As often as not, it is the quaintness of a title or a book's potential interest as a record of past tastes and customs that draws one to an old cookbook. Who, while rummaging through a cardboard box at a jumble sale, could spot a book called *Open Sesame: The Way of a Cook with a Can* and not be tempted to thumb through it? Other titles from the 1920s and 1930s, like *Picnics for Motorists*, are less eye-catching, but equally evocative of a vanished era. Cookbooks of the period also tended to contain such curiosities as 'additional pages on Australian tinned meats, soups and fish' or a section on making soups in a haybox.

## DISAPPOINTING FOOD

As in all periods of history, it was possible to eat very well, but it was all too easy to eat badly, not only in poorer homes, but also in expensive restaurants and at exclusive dinner parties. The reasons for this were largely social. Many middle-class women who had grown up assuming that they would employ a cook when they got married found that this was no longer possible. There still were cooks prepared to work for £120 a year and traditional 'perks' in a grand house, but in smaller houses and flats people had to make do with a maid of all work, whose culinary skill could be decidedly limited.

The skill of many cooks was apparently not much greater. Cooks advertising their services defined themselves as 'good plain cooks' or 'chef-trained'. The problem with the 'good plains', according to Ruth Lowinsky, author of *Lovely Food*, a rare limited edition of 1931, was that they thought they were 'entitled to boil everything and serve with a garnish of water'. The 'chef-trained', on the other hand, 'is quite unable to roast or grill meat, though she can send up the most marvellous looking mousses. It is only by their position on the menu and the fact that they taste vaguely of sugar or salt that you know whether they be made of lobsters or strawberries'.

In general, both housewives and employers of cooks set their sights too high. After the privations of

World War I too many people still aspired to re-create Edwardian meals at the Ritz, when Escoffier reigned supreme. Virginia Woolf in *A Room of One's Own* gives a splendid picture of a grand feast of the time, including 'sole, sunk in a deep dish, over which the College cook had spread a counterpane of the whitest cream, save that it was branded here and there with brown spots like the spots on the flanks of a doe'. Alas, one could pay large sums of money to have spotted counterpanes spread over rubbery fillets of ill-cooked fish.

In the end many accepted the fact that God had created Frenchmen to practise *haute cuisine* and lesser mortals should leave well alone. A French cook was a great status symbol in an age when people would refuse an invitation to a palatial country house because the cooking there was so awful. One of the great chefs of the period was Marcel Boulestin. The fame of his restaurant made his books the last word on French cooking for the English.

However, the wise English cook stuck to good old English roasts, puddings and pies. The art of cake-baking was also in good health – fierce competition at village fêtes kept everyone up to the mark. Scones were a reliable standby and the English breakfast was still a sacrosanct and nourishing institution.

The virtues of traditional local recipes were given a great boost by Florence White's *Good Things in England*. With its wealth of historical research, it is still quoted by today's writers and it has been reprinted. Another book which has received much praise in modern times, and from no less an authority than Elizabeth David, is Mrs C. F. Leyel's *The Gentle Art of Cookery*, published in 1929.

### INVALUABLE BOOKS

Anything by Mrs Leyel is well worth buying if you come across it. She dealt with many aspects of cooking: some, like *Meals on a Tray*, are obviously dated, but in *Diet and Common Sense* she approached the subject of food from a very modern point of view. On the other hand, a book like *Herbal delights: Tisanes, Syrups, Confections, Electuaries, Robs, Juleps, Vinegars and Conserves* might tax most people's culinary vocabulary today, but then doubtless it did when it was first published.

When a young woman was setting up home, the book she was most likely to receive to help her on her way was still the encyclopaedic *Mrs Beeton's Book of Household Management*. As this made rather daunting reading, there were simpler 'Cookbooks for Brides' and a great many 'hostess' books. *The Perfect Hostess*, by Rose Henniker Heaton, is a hilarious account of the pretensions of the period. For instance, the need to show off with lots of fiddly canapés, hors d'oeuvres, savouries and soufflés meant that the main elements of the meal were often sadly neglected. Also the cachet of having printed menu cards could be more important than the menu itself.

Many girls were prepared for the roles of wife, cook and hostess at cookery school or a college of domestic science. Some of the latter published their own recipe books. These could be very old-fashioned in their use of French distinctions between entrées, relevés and entremets and their insistence on the need to offer both a thick and a clear soup. Watery consommés got many a dinner party off to a dismal start:

> The consommé, wan as Elizabeth Barrett,
> Washes over a drowning carrot,

as Ogden Nash put it.

Of course, those who regularly included Consommé à la Julienne, Sole Normande and Angels on Horseback on their menus made up a very small percentage of the population.

### BUDGET COOKERY

Meals for most people were meat and two veg garnished with water, if they were lucky; rissoles, fishcakes and tins of sardines if they were not. And they, too, had their recipe books. 'Every atom of food left from a meal should be placed on clean plates in a clean, cool larder, covered from dust and flies, and when ordering the meal for the next day the caterer should see how she can work in the remains of the new material.' This sound advice came from Mrs C. S. Peel O.B.E., who, having written for the Ministry of Food during the War, became the doyenne of economic cookery writers in the 1920s. Daily and evening papers also gave useful recipes and tips on domestic economy, as did a number of

◀ *A selection of inter-war cookery books. Books by Mrs Beeton – 'the housewife's Guide, Philosopher and Friend' – now included a few coloured illustrations. Eating without Fears is full of entertaining anecdotes.*

▲ *McDougall's – a household name then as now – promoted their flour not only through adverts in women's magazines but also by producing free cookery booklets with recipes which made use of their products.*

women's magazines. *Good Housekeeping*, indeed, produced its own series of recipe books.

Cooking was not made any easier by the fact that a vast number of people found themselves having to use gas or electricity for the first time in their lives. Booklets of instructions on using the cooker were followed by a selection of basic recipes, as in *Good Things to Cook and Eat* from Revo Electric Cookers.

Some manufacturers brought out full-scale recipe books as well, as did the makers of well-known food products like Tate & Lyle, Oxo, Atora Suet and Brown & Polson Corn Flour. The best-seller of them all was probably *McDougall's Cookery Book*, still going strong today, particularly in the north of England.

### FORMING A COLLECTION

Recipe booklets and other advertising material can be found very cheaply at ephemera fairs, but interest in cookery books of the period is growing and they may soon become more scarce. There are as yet very few second-hand booksellers who specialize in old cookbooks, but you are bound to find something in almost every large second-hand bookshop and also at jumble sales. The problem is to find books in good condition; most will unfortunately bear evidence of having been used in the kitchen.

Collecting is bound to be a little haphazard, but you may find yourself drawn to one particularly attractive series of books, for example those by Dorothy Allhusen or Ambrose Heath's 'Good Food' series published by Faber. Another thing collectors have to decide is whether they want all those hand-written recipes and cuttings from news-papers that you find on the blank pages at the back of so many cookbooks. Some find them fascinating, others have no time for them because they detract from the value of the book, unless, of course, they should happen to be by somebody famous!

◀ *A range of brand-name cookery booklets produced by food and equipment manufacturers. The* New Radiation Recipe Book *is less ominous than it sounds – the Radiation Group were the makers of gas cookers. Elizabeth Craig was a well-known cookery writer of the period.*

# INDEX

# INDEX

# INDEX

## PICTURE CREDITS